ZIMBABWE

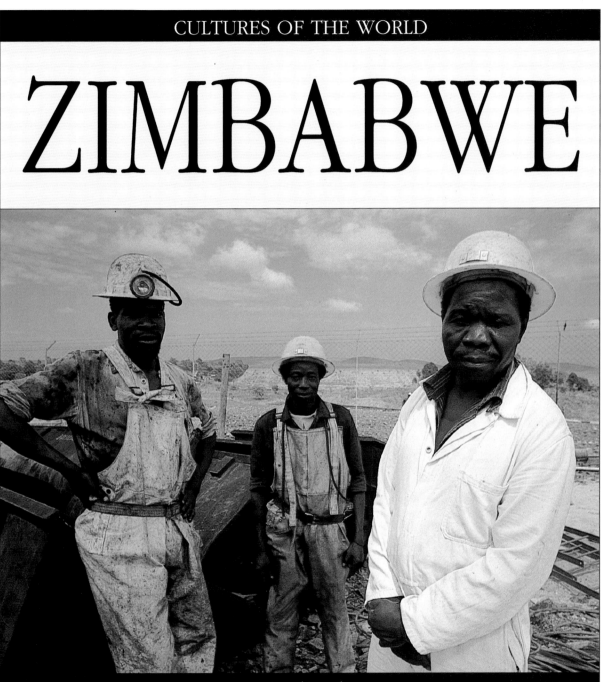

Sean Sheehan

MARSHALL CAVENDISH
New York • London • Sydney

Reference edition published 1994 by
Marshall Cavendish Corporation
2415 Jerusalem Avenue
P.O. Box 587
North Bellmore
New York 11710

© Times Editions Pte Ltd 1993

Originated and designed by
Times Books International, an imprint of
Times Editions Pte Ltd

Printed in Malaysia

Library of Congress Cataloging-in-Publication Data:
Sheehan, Sean,
   Zimbabwe / Sean Sheehan.
      p. cm.—(Cultures Of The World)
   Includes bibliographical references and index.
   Summary: Describes the geography, history,
government, economy, and culture of Zimbabwe.
   ISBN 1-85435-577-5
   1. Zimbabwe—Juvenile literature [1. Zimbabwe.]
I. Title. II. Series.
DT2889.S54 1993
968.91—dc20   92–38751
                     CIP
                     AC

Cultures of the World

Editorial Director	Shirley Hew
Managing Editor	Shova Loh
Editors	Leonard Lau
	Tan Kok Eng
	Michael Spilling
	Sue Sismondo
Picture Editor	Yee May Kaung
Production	Edmund Lam
Design	Tuck Loong
	Ronn Yeo
	Felicia Wong
	Loo Chuan Ming
Illustrators	Jimmy Kang
	Kelvin Sim
	Philip Lim
MCC Editorial Director	Evelyn M. Fazio

INTRODUCTION

ONCE THE FABLED LAND of the Queen of Sheba and King Solomon's mines, the contemporary state of Zimbabwe continues to excite wonder. Victoria Falls, the ruins of a medieval civilization, and the largest concentration of wild elephants in the world are some of the sights found in the country.

The human landscape is equally fascinating in its own way. Despite a colonial past that treated the overwhelming majority of the country's people as inferior to the minority white rulers, modern Zimbabwe has a unique culture that allows blacks and whites to live together peacefully.

After many tragic years of struggle, Zimbabwe has emerged as one of the most progressive states in the whole of Africa. Its culture, especially in the arts, is vibrant and independent.

This book, part of the *Cultures of the World* series, seeks to help readers understand the nation of Zimbabwe better.

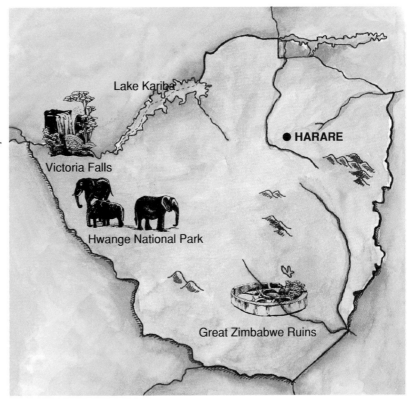

Lake Kariba

● HARARE

Victoria Falls

Hwange National Park

Great Zimbabwe Ruins

CONTENTS

A traditional dwelling in Zimbabwe is decorated with geometric patterns.

CONTENTS

A cheetah waits patiently in an open plain in Zimbabwe for its prey. The fastest land animal in the world over short distances, the cheetah can attain a speed of at least 60 miles per hour.

GEOGRAPHY

ZIMBABWE is situated in the southern half of the African continent. Covering 156,304 square miles, it is about the size of California. It is bounded on all sides by land, with Zambia to the north, Botswana to the southwest, and South Africa to the south. Mozambique is to the east, separating Zimbabwe from the Indian Ocean. The country's geography has helped make Zimbabwe one of Africa's most prosperous nations, and the richness of its natural attractions is one of the country's main assets.

Opposite: **Nearly one mile wide, Victoria Falls drops more than 300 feet. It is one-and-a-half times as wide as Niagara Falls and twice as high.**

Below: **This undulating terrain lies in the High Veld, a broad ridge that covers about a fourth of the country.**

THE SHAPE OF ZIMBABWE

Much of Zimbabwe includes part of a great plateau that dominates southern Africa. The plateau, shaped like a vast upside-down saucer, tilts upward toward the east, and has areas of varying heights.

A high area, known as the High Veld, takes the form of a ridge that runs from the southwest to the northeast. This is the backbone of the country. Here, the land is at least 3,960 feet above sea level, ideal for European-style farming. On each side of the High Veld lies the wider plateau of the Middle Veld, with an elevation between 2,970 and 3,960 feet. Below this, especially in the south, is the Low Veld, where the land is never above 2,970 feet. The Low Veld is hot and dry, and has some of the poorest agriculture in the country.

THE MATOPOS HILLS

The Matopos Hills, formed of granite and gneiss, are billions of years old. Caves there were home to the earliest human inhabitants of Zimbabwe. Paintings that go back some 2,000 years are found on the walls.

The Matopos Hills are situated 310 miles south of Victoria Falls, near the city of Bulawayo. More recent inhabitants to this part of Zimbabwe are the Ndebele people, who came and settled there from their Zulu homelands in the first half of the 19th century. For the Ndebele, the hills and caves of the Matopos are regarded as sacred. When their king, Mzilikazi, died, his remains were sealed in a hillside tomb. Cecil Rhodes, the leader and financier of the first white settlers of Zimbabwe, is also buried in this area.

Geographically, the Matopos Hills are interesting for the unusual granite outcrops that can be found in the area. Known as kopjes or kops, these isolated blocks of stones have been shaped into weird and wonderful formations that resemble animals and faces of people. Sometimes they are precariously balanced one on top of the other, or just scattered around as if they had been thrown away by some mighty giant. Mzilikazi named the area Matobos ("the baldheaded ones") after the granite masses, and the word was later corrupted to Matopos.

The undulating landscape of the High Veld is broken up by intrusions of hard rock. The Great Dyke, over 300 miles long and 6 miles wide, is one notable example of this feature.

Formed by the solidified magma of volcanic activity millions of years ago, the Great Dyke contains rich seams of chromite, asbestos, nickel, and platinum. It runs through the center of Zimbabwe, and its mineral-rich content is one of the country's most valuable resources.

The Matopos Hills are another example. The hills formed by these intrusions are, however, not as high as the mountainous Eastern Highlands, where Inyangani, at 8,560 feet, rises as the highest mountain in Zimbabwe. This is the most spectacular part of the country.

RIVERS

There are two main rivers in Zimbabwe: the Limpopo in the south and the Zambezi in the north. Both of them help to define the country's international borders. The Limpopo divides Zimbabwe from the republic of South Africa, while the Zambezi marks the country's boundary with Zambia.

The Zambezi flows for 1,650 miles and is one of the longest rivers in Africa. Only the Nile, the Zaire, and the Niger rivers are longer. After the Zambezi's dramatic 300-foot drop into a mile-wide chasm at Victoria Falls, the river flows through the Kariba Gorge, where its waters are harnessed for electricity in a dam. Lake Kariba is one of the largest artificial lakes in the world, covering over 2,000 square miles. The dam water feeds a power station that supplies electricity to both Zimbabwe and Zambia, for the lake is shared by both countries. The enormous mass of water creates so much pressure that slight earthquakes have been recorded in the vicinity of the dam.

Above: **Early dawn by the Zambezi River.**

Opposite: **Severely weathered by wind and water, these balancing rocks of granite and gneiss are a notable feature of Zimbabwe's landscape.**

The largest artificial lake in the world after Egypt's Lake Nasser, Lake Kariba was formed by the damming of the Zambezi River. Many river dwellers had to be resettled when the lake was created, and countless animals had to be rescued when the waters flooded their habitats. Today, animal and bird life flourish on the shores of the lake.

The Limpopo is 1,100 miles long and flows up from South Africa, forming that country's borders with Botswana and Zimbabwe. The 19th-century English poet Rudyard Kipling described it as the "great grey-green, greasy Limpopo River, all set about with fever-trees." Until the recent relaxation of relations between South Africa and Zimbabwe, the river border between the two countries was filled with steel netting. This was to catch the floating mines that South Africa feared would be released by black nationalist guerrillas operating from Zimbabwe. Today, the river border is still heavily guarded, but this has not prevented young Zimbabwean workers from crossing into South Africa for work in the gold and diamond mines there.

VICTORIA FALLS

Victoria Falls, situated on the Zambezi River, is one of the largest falls in the world. Over 150 million years old, it was created at a time when volcanic lava from the earth's crust cooled and contracted to form crevices. These later expanded due to the influence of the flooding river. The resulting gorge now receives this vast cascade of water from the Zambezi River as it tumbles into the chasm.

The tremendous power of the water falling more than 300 feet creates a terrific roar that can be heard from a distance of 25 miles. In addition to the noise, clouds of spray rise into the air and create a broad mist that is visible nearly 4 miles away. The African name for the falls is Mosi-oa-tunya, or "the smoke that thunders."

David Livingstone, the 19th-century Scottish explorer and missionary, is often referred to as the discoverer of Victoria Falls. He first saw the falls in 1855 and named them in honor of Britain's Queen Victoria. It is more correct to credit Livingstone with being the first white person to set eyes on the falls, as he was taken there by local Africans to view the spectacle. Traveling along the Zambezi River, his astonishment at the phenomenon is recorded in his diary. He describes the falls as so impressive that it "must have been gazed on by angels in their flight."

CLIMATE

A clump of bamboo thrives along the banks of a river. Zimbabwe has a rainy and a dry season. The rains fall during the summer months and help keep the vegetation lush and green.

The climate is affected by the country's different altitudes, with the low-lying areas being the hottest. October is the warmest month, when average highs reach 86°F on the Low Veld and 72°F on the High Veld. The summer season lasts from September to April. Wintertime, from May to August, is coldest on the High Veld. Although the nights are cold, the days are usually warm and sunny.

The cooler temperatures on the High Veld, combined with regular rainfall, help produce an ideal climate for the farmers there. The subtropical conditions provide a perfect environment for grass to grow tall and for raising cattle. The main towns of Harare and Bulawayo have an average of eight hours of sunshine every day throughout the year.

Rainfall is heaviest in the Eastern Highlands, where the monsoon winds that have crossed from the Indian Ocean meet the mountainous highlands. The consequent heavy rains help create the lush vegetation in this part of Zimbabwe.

In the low-lying areas, the climate is dry and hot and not conducive to farming. The grass is coarse, and only bush and thorny trees manage to prosper in the harsh and dry heat. The lack of sufficient rainfall means that growing crops on a commercial basis is often unprofitable. Nevertheless, there has been success in irrigating the Low Veld in the southeast. Land that was once suitable only for ranching is now proving to be agriculturally lucrative.

LANDSCAPES AND VEGETATION

Apart from the highlands in the eastern part of the country, the countryside is generally flat. It is not monotonous, however, because the scenery changes from one area to another. An hour's drive will take one from bushland to tobacco fields or corn prairies, and a day's drive would traverse the entire length or breadth of the country.

The landscape of the Eastern Highlands is different from the rest of the countryside. The mountains and rivers, the timber plantations, and green valleys give an Alpine look, but the names of the mountain ranges are unmistakably African: Nyanga, Vumba, and Chimanimani. Once a place of refuge for tribes fleeing from trouble, the highlands now attract vacationers seeking outdoor activities such as fishing, hiking, and climbing.

Much of Zimbabwe is tropical grassland. The forests are limited to the evergreen trees along the Eastern Highlands and the savanna woodland in the west. Various species of brachystegia, a tall hardwood, can be found in the Middle Veld and the High Veld. Baobab

The baobab tree grows in the valleys of the Zambezi and Limpopo rivers. The fiber of the bark can be used for making rope and cloth.

("BAY-oh-bahb") trees are found in the drier areas of the south and southwest. The baobab is a strange-looking tree. Its huge barrel-shaped trunk, sometimes measuring as much as 40 feet in circumference, appears too large for its spidery crown. The baobab's trunk is adapted for storing water. In the vicinity of Victoria Falls, there is a famous baobab tree, reported to be over 1,000 years old, that bears the signature of David Livingstone.

ANIMAL LIFE

A wide array of animal life can be found in Zimbabwe, especially in the national parks and reserves. Elephants, lions, cheetahs, zebras, and giraffes are common on land, while crocodiles and hippopotamuses abound in the water. Antelopes are also easily spotted, and Zimbabwe is home to many different species. Klipspringers are one species that feed together in family groups and warn each other with a shrill whistle if they sense a predator. Another type of antelope found in Zimbabwe is the gnu, or wildebeest, a very fast animal that travels in groups from a dozen to a few hundred. The kudu is a larger, lightly striped antelope that stands about 4 feet at the shoulder. The male of the species has long, corkscrew-like horns that can grow to as much as 3 feet.

HWANGE NATIONAL PARK

The largest national park in Zimbabwe is Hwange, covering nearly 6,000 square miles in the northwest corner of the country. The next most important park is Mana Pools, some 248 miles north of Harare, where the increasingly rare black rhinoceros is found.

The Hwange National Park has about 20,000 elephants, and the number is growing at a rate of 5% a year. There is also a wide range of other animals, including 413 species of birds. The land itself forms the most easterly side of the vast Kalahari Desert that covers two-thirds of neighboring Botswana. The national park was formed in 1929 because no other use for the land could be found. Parts of it had formerly been a Ndebele hunting reserve. Today, the only hunters are tourists who take part in controlled safari hunts. Quotas for trophy animals are set by a government department.

The Hwange National Park provides accommodation for all budgets. Between the months of August and October, visitors flock in to watch the game.

Aardvarks and zorillas, though a long way apart in dictionaries, live side by side in Zimbabwe. The aardvark lives by eating insects. Its long and narrow snout is used for foraging close to the ground, while its large donkey-like ears are on the alert for any sounds of danger. The zorilla, or African polecat, like the aardvark, is a nocturnal creature, but its diet is more varied. It feeds on small mammals, birds, and invertebrates. Like the American skunk, it excretes a foul smell to repel predators.

Snakes that are dangerous to humans include boomslangs, mambas, and the black-necked cobra. The mamba is one of the world's most venomous snakes. There are four species: three types of green mambas and one black. The black mamba is very fast, and will chase its prey before injecting its powerful nerve toxin. The green mambas are not so aggressive and, unlike the black species, will not usually attack mammals, preferring lizards, eggs, and small birds.

Opposite top: **Large numbers of zebras and antelopes are still found in Zimbabwe. Although they are the favorite prey of lions, the antelope can often outrun the lion and the zebra can deliver a fatal kick if it is attacked.**

Opposite bottom: **Elephants in a game reserve. Zimbabwe has some 70,000 elephants, twice the estimated amount that the country can support. As a result, managed killing or culling is practiced. It is argued that this practice is not totally against the elephants' interests, as it guarantees more food for the survivors.**

Ivory on display in a shop in Zimbabwe. Since the ban, the price of ivory has fallen dramatically, and poachers no longer have the incentive to organize large-scale elephant hunts.

THE ELEPHANT AND IVORY ISSUE

The number of elephants in Africa has declined by half over the last 10 years, mainly as a result of intensive poaching. Ivory tusks have been much sought after in Hong Kong, China, and Japan. The prices paid were high enough to finance large-scale and highly professional teams of poachers. In 1989, after many years of protest and lobbying by animal rights groups, an international agreement was reached to ban the trade and sale of African elephant ivory. Zimbabwe, however, is strongly opposed to the ban, and argues that the agreement on international trade should not apply to every country. The issue is hotly disputed.

What is not in dispute is the fascinating appeal that elephants have for people. Tales of their habits have become folklore. They are said to have amazing memories. It is also believed that they become ashamed after killing a human, and would cover up the body with leaves and grass. What is a fact is their deep regard for funeral rites. They spend a long time disposing of their own dead, and remain near the burying grounds for some time after. When alive and well, a full-grown adult eats 375 pounds of food a day.

TOWNSCAPES

Zimbabwe's cities, towns, and villages are remarkably tidy and well-groomed. Streets are usually wide, a legacy of the days when they were planned to enable an ox and wagon team to turn around. Visitors are often surprised at the colorful flowers and trees that decorate the roadsides, and the way town parks have the town's name planted in foxgloves and marigolds.

16

HARARE The capital of Zimbabwe was originally named Salisbury. When Zimbabwe became independent in 1980, the capital's name was changed to Harare.

Harare, the capital of Zimbabwe, was founded in 1890. Situated at an altitude of 4,865 feet, it has a temperate climate.

Harare's population is still below 1 million, but it is growing as more people from the countryside seek employment there. The broad streets of the capital are characteristic of most Zimbabwean towns. Because of the pleasant year-round climate, many parks and open spaces are filled with flowers. Even streets are bordered with flowering trees in the summer. There is, however, not enough jobs for everyone who comes to the capital to look for one. Harare also has its share of shanty dwellings, where poor families live.

BULAWAYO The second largest city in Zimbabwe, Bulawayo has a population of half a million. It is an important industrial center because the surrounding area is rich in mineral deposits. There are a number of large mines. Also, because of its transportation links with Victoria Falls and the national parks, the city attracts a large number of tourists. Historically, Bulawayo is important because it was the center of what was once called Matabeleland—homeland to the Ndebele people, the most important tribal group in Zimbabwe after the majority Shona people.

HISTORY

EVIDENCE OF A DISTINCTIVE Stone Age culture in Zimbabwe goes back 500,000 years. The early peoples were hunters and food gatherers. They later settled down in communities.

The first non-Africans to reach the land between the Limpopo and the Zambezi rivers were Moslem traders, who were active along the east coast as early as the 10th century. After the Arabs, came the Portuguese, but it was the British in the 19th century who made a permanent impression. They expropriated the land and named it Rhodesia. Only after years of violent struggle did the country return to black rule in 1980. Rhodesia became known as Zimbabwe, named after a powerful local civilization that flourished during the 14th and 15th centuries.

Above: **Cave paintings at Matopos. Matopos was home to the Bushmen, who lived there more than 2,000 years ago. On the walls of the caves and shelters, they painted colorful pictures of animals and people.**

Opposite: **Wall structures of Great Zimbabwe, once a thriving center of commerce and trade. Porcelain from China has been found in Great Zimbabwe's medieval ruins, evidence of a sophisticated trading network.**

EARLY HISTORY

Some people believe that Africa is the birthplace of the human race. Stone tools have been found that date back some 2 million years. In ancient Zimbabwe, early people used basalt to fashion hammers and spearheads. The pigments from the iron contained in the basalt rock allowed cave paintings to be made in shades of yellow, red, and brown. Such paintings are still well preserved.

It is thought that the San (Bushmen), who still live in the Kalahari Desert, are the last descendants of the original inhabitants of southern and central Africa. They were driven into the desert by the Bantu-speaking peoples when they migrated to this region.

Linguistic evidence points to early Bantu culture reaching Zimbabwe around A.D. 300. Some 500 years later, the stone foundations to Great Zimbabwe were laid. By the 10th century, gold and copper were exported from over a thousand mines. They were passed through Mozambique to Arab traders.

GREAT ZIMBABWE

The stone structures known as Great Zimbabwe date back to the 9th century. They are the largest and most important buildings constructed by humans in southern Africa before modern times.

GRANDEUR IN STONE

The architecture of Great Zimbabwe can be divided into three sections: the Hill Complex, the Great Enclosure, and the Valley Complex.

The Hill Complex is a steep 330-foot-high granite hill dotted with ruins, including, near the summit, a high space ringed by walls. This may have been the king's headquarters, or perhaps the seat of a royal spirit medium. It contained stone bird figures of the king's chief oracles. They remained there until plundered by Europeans at the end of the 19th century. The bird's name was Shiri ya Mwari, the Bird of God. It was through its cries that the spiritual advisers to the king would communicate with their ancestors.

The Great Enclosure is a massive elliptical ruin 30 feet in height and 800 feet in circumference. Thought to be the court of the king's wives, the Great Enclosure has a conical tower, but the purpose and meaning of this tower remain unknown.

The Valley Complex has a number of smaller ruins, which indicates that the whole area was the social and political capital of Zimbabwe during the 14th and 15th centuries. Evidence of gold smelting and an elaborate drainage system all point to a prosperous community. Centuries later, gold was found in some of the ruins. A group of early European looters even founded their own company, called the Rhodesian Ancient Ruins Company.

The Great Zimbabwe ruins are the remains of a medieval African civilization that expressed its grandeur in granite. It follows the basic style of the mud-and-thatch villages that mostly made up its capital city of 10,000 people. The civilization extended over most of what is now Zimbabwe. The basis of its wealth was gold. The precious metal was smelted in Great Zimbabwe and sent through Mozambique to the coast, where it began its sea journey across the Indian Ocean. Manufactured goods, especially cotton, were traded for the gold.

The Shona word "zimbabwe" means royal court. More than 200 stone buildings were built as the homes and power bases for local kings, or the representatives of royal command. The largest of all is the one that a 16th-century Portuguese merchant explorer described as "a very curious and well-constructed building in which no cement can be seen." Four hundred years later, the ruins are still remarkable and impressive. They attract the largest number of tourists after Victoria Falls.

The Portuguese introduced Christianity to Zimbabwe, for when they controlled Mwana-Mutapa they insisted on conversion to Christianity through their Dominican priests.

MWANA-MUTAPA ("RAVAGER OF THE LANDS")

Sometime in the first half of the 15th century, Great Zimbabwe was abandoned and power moved north. There, the king set about conquering neighboring lands and, in the process, earned the title of Mwana-Mutapa or "Ravager of the Lands."

Mwana-Mutapa became the title of a dynasty that was to last until the 19th century. When the Portuguese began exploring this part of Africa, they misheard the title as Monomotapa, which then entered the historical records as "the great kingdom with the key to trade in gold."

An early attempt to invade the country led to failure but, eventually, in 1630, the Portuguese were able to install their own puppet king in the north of Zimbabwe. They ruled a large part of the country through force.

In the south of Zimbabwe, the land of the Rozvi, a more independent spirit had prevailed. The Rozvi rulers built their own "zimbabwes," and impressive ruins can be found near the city of Bulawayo. In 1663, the Rozvi formed an alliance with Mwana-Mutapa and defeated the Portuguese. Despite their defeat, the Portuguese maintained a trading presence in the country.

It was some 300 years later that the British arrived. They had a more lasting influence than the Portuguese. But, in the meantime, Zimbabwe became home to a group of Africans from the south, the Ndebele.

THE NDEBELE

The Ndebele, who are concentrated in the southwest of Zimbabwe, arrived in the first half of the 19th century. Until then, the Shona had lived throughout Zimbabwe and, apart from the conflict with the Portuguese, their way of life had continued undisturbed for centuries. However, to the south of their land, in what is now South Africa, the rise of the Zulu warrior Shaka had a profound effect on Zimbabwe.

As Shaka's army grew in power and influence, Zulu clans had to accept his authority, or find somewhere else to live. Pressure to move also came from a land shortage that had been intensified by white settlers moving into South Africa. One clan that did choose exile rather than submission moved north into Zimbabwe, pursued for a long time by Shaka's warriors. They eventually established themselves at Bulawayo in the 1840s.

These people, the Ndebele, were forced at first to survive by stealing cattle and raiding their neighbors. They also established their own cultural identity despite being surrounded by the dominant Shona. Eventually, as their strength grew, the Ndebele were able to subdue neighboring Shona clans. Their warrior origins helped them to establish and maintain a system of tribute payments from the Shona. In return for gifts of cattle, these ex-Zulus were able to offer the protection of their professional army. By 1870, when Lobengula became their new king, they were a permanent and powerful force of cattle farmers and warriors.

Ndebele influence extended well beyond their capital at Bulawayo. Anyone attempting to move into Zimbabwe would have to make peace with, or defeat, Lobengula's army. This fact soon became obvious to the first white people, who were irresistibly drawn to Zimbabwe by stories of the countless gold mines to be found there.

A Ndebele medicine man. The Ndebele were mighty warriors of Zulu origin. It took some years before Cecil Rhodes felt confident enough to take on the Ndebele in battle.

LOBENGULA

When 19th-century Englishmen and others were keen to secure concessions for the right to mine for gold in Zimbabwe, they went to Lobengula, the undisputed king of the land.

Lobengula was no fool. He tried his best to contain the greed and ambitions of the white entrepreneurs who were showing much interest in the land he ruled. He did not recklessly sign away valuable rights, but was tricked and duped by wily men who came to his camp pretending to have his interests at heart.

A missionary named Moffat won his trust and claimed to have Lobengula's signature to a treaty that forbade anyone but the British to negotiate with him. Then Lobengula was tricked into granting a mining concession to all minerals in his "kingdom, principalities and domains, together with full power to do all things that they may deem necessary to win and procure same."

The Ndebele king was under the impression that no more than 10 Europeans would ever mine in his land at any one time, and that they would be subject to the law and authority of the Ndebele.

These conditions, however, never found their way onto paper. When Lobengula found out, he tried to cancel the agreement. It was too late; the British government had, on the strength of this phony concession, granted the British South Africa Company the right to enter the country and undertake its business.

After three years, it was clear that the British intended to make the land their own. Lobengula was under pressure from his own people to fight, although he knew that the assegais (wooden spears tipped with metal) of his young warriors were no match for the machine gun.

The battle came when the British found an excuse to attack the Ndebele. Lobengula was forced to set fire to Bulawayo and flee. He died some time later, a very disillusioned king.

Financier and empire builder of British South Africa, Cecil Rhodes was a leading proponent of British colonialism in Africa in the late 19th century.

CECIL RHODES

For nearly a hundred years, Zimbabwe was known to the world as Rhodesia, named after an Englishman who described his philosophy as one of "philanthropy plus 5%." He worked with great missionary zeal to bring what he called civilization to the Africans, while at the same time amassing a huge fortune. His ambition was to "paint the map red" (referring to the practice of coloring red those parts of the world incorporated into the British Empire), and build a railway line from the tip of South Africa to Egypt in the north.

Rhodes was the son of an English priest who, at the age of 17, left to join his brother's cotton farm in South Africa. He later made his fortune by gaining the rights to diamond fields there. Within a few years, he owned the rights to 90% of the world's diamonds.

Rhodes then set his sights on Zimbabwe, after listening to the tales of adventurers about large reserves of gold in the land across the Limpopo River. He formed the British South Africa Company. In 1890, he organized, but did not lead, a group of 200 men who crossed the Limpopo to occupy the land. He justified the invasion on the grounds that Lobengula had given him full rights to the territory.

Rhodes's name lives on, no longer in the name of a country, but in the scholarships he established at Oxford University.

25

The hoisting of the Union Jack at Fort Salisbury in 1890 was a significant event, marking British occupation and, later, colonization of Zimbabwe.

THE 1890 INVASION

The "Pioneer Column" that crossed the Limpopo and marched into southern Zimbabwe consisted of 200 prospectors, backed up by a private army of 500 armed policemen. The prospectors were each promised 15 gold-prospecting claims and 3,000 acres of land. Once over the Limpopo River, they established Fort Victoria, now the oldest town in Zimbabwe. Continuing their journey, the column kept to the east of Lobengula's territory. Unlike the Shona, the Ndebele did not accept their presence.

Soon, the column came to rest near a hill that was once the domain of a local chief named Harare. The prospectors raised the Union Jack and declared the place Fort Salisbury, named after the British prime minister of the time. A boundary line was drawn between the land of the Ndebele and that of the Shona.

It was soon discovered that the new territory was not as rich in gold as previously thought. The next best way to make a living was by farming. The best Ndebele land was appropriated after Lobengula was defeated. In 1895, the land of the Monomotapa and the Rozvi became known as Rhodesia.

THE FIRST CHIMURENGA

In 1896, the Ndebele rose in revolt. They were joined by the Shona, who had also seen some of their best land stolen by the prospectors once they realized the gold supplies were insufficient to make their fortunes. The rebellion became known as the First Chimurenga, derived from a Shona word meaning "war of liberation."

Rhodes was able to use Western technology to his advantage. The hand-cranked Gatling and the fully automatic Maxim machine guns were powerful weapons at the time. Cannon were also used to defeat the insurgents. When the rebels took refuge in caves, sticks of dynamite were used to force them out.

Later, Rhodes made peace with the Ndebele *indunas* (headmen), with a promise to return occupied land. The promise was never kept. Left to fight on by themselves, the Shona rebels were systematically defeated and their leaders executed.

Ndebele children ride on cattle to school. Besides being raised for livestock, cattle provide a means of transportation.

Before the uprising, the Ndebele and Shona people possessed around 300,000 head of cattle. After their defeat, the number was below 15,000. The British took the Ndebele cattle, claiming they had been the personal possession of Lobengula. But the cattle really belonged to the whole community.

THE SEEDS OF REVOLUTION

Rhodes's company, the British South Africa Company, ran what was then called Rhodesia until the 1920s. In 1923, it became Southern Rhodesia, a self-governing colony within the British Empire, but it made no difference to the vast majority of black Africans. The right to vote was based on British citizenship.

The traditional communal farming economy of the blacks was destroyed in order to create large farms for the whites. The dispossessed blacks were employed as cheap labor, or left on reservations of poor and infertile land. A person could not move from the place of work without permission from the employer, and pass laws made it easy to control the local population.

After World War II, the situation deteriorated as the white population increased. Large numbers of new European settlers were attracted to the idea of making a prosperous living out of farming, especially the growing of tobacco. New laws further dispossessed the black population of land.

WORKING IN THE MINES

The gold reserves were not as rich as the prospectors imagined, and a profit was made by paying very low wages. When blacks were reluctant to work the mines, they were rounded up by force and compelled to work in a system known as "chibaro." The workers christened individual mines with their own names, indicating clearly how they felt about the experience.

Mtshalwana ("mit-shahl-WAH-NA"): you will fight one another
Sigebengu ("sig-erh-BENG-OO"): bosses are villains
Makombera ("makh-ohm-BERH-rah"): you are closed in
Maplanki ("mah-PLAHN-ki"): planks for punishment

The years after World War II also saw the growth of nationalist aspirations, not just in Rhodesia but all across Africa. Despite strong opposition from nationalists, in 1953 a federation was formed between Southern Rhodesia (Zimbabwe), Northern Rhodesia (Zambia), and Nyasaland (Malawi). In 1963, the federation was dissolved, with Northern Rhodesia and Nyasaland only months from independence. In Southern Rhodesia, however, the white population dug their heels in and resisted any calls for liberalization.

BLACK NATIONALISM

Black nationalism made itself felt in the 1950s when a bus boycott was organized in the capital against fare increases. In 1957, the African National Congress (ANC) was formed, calling for "the national unity of all inhabitants of this country in true partnership regardless of race, color, and creed." Strikes and marches were held. The ANC was consequently banned.

Joshua Nkomo, the nationalist leader of ZAPU, inspects his forces.

The repression only intensified black opposition to white rule. Opposition spread across the cities, and the army responded to a strike in Bulawayo by killing 18 demonstrators.

In 1961, the Zimbabwe African People's Union (ZAPU) was formed, but there were differences of opinion over the best way to combat white rule. A couple of years later, the Zimbabwe African National Union (ZANU) was also formed. A leading member of ZANU was Robert Mugabe.

The Unilateral Declaration of Independence (UDI) was signed by Ian Smith on November 11, 1965. It gave Rhodesia complete authority over its own affairs.

"We have struck a blow for the preservation of justice, civilization, and Christianity, and in the spirit of this belief we have this day assumed our sovereign independence. God bless you all."
—The Prime Minister of Rhodesia, announcing UDI.

INDEPENDENCE—FOR WHITES ONLY

As most of Africa gained self-rule, the white rulers of Rhodesia became more alarmed at the prospect of losing their power and privileges. In 1965, the government declared the country's refusal to be bound by Britain and its determination to preserve white rule. This was the Unilateral Declaration of Independence (UDI), announced by Prime Minister Ian Smith.

The British government called the UDI an illegal act, and sanctions were adopted by the United Nations. However, the sanctions failed to put pressure on white Rhodesia. This was because they were never strongly enforced. In fact, seven years after the UDI, Rhodesia's exports were actually higher than they had been in 1965.

Rhodesia did attempt to introduce a new constitution that would have given extremely limited rights to the black population, but when they sought approval from the country's black majority, they were met with a resounding rejection. The effect gave a boost to the black nationalist movement. The white government responded by introducing more repressive legislation, including South African-style apartheid laws: segregated public facilities and tougher pass laws.

Armed resistance to white rule had begun in 1966, but both ZANU and ZAPU found it difficult to fight government troops that were better organized and financed. But by December 1972, a new phase in the struggle for liberation began that proved to be more effective. This was the Second Chimurenga.

THE SECOND CHIMURENGA

In 1972, armed resistance to white rule began in earnest. Numerous attacks were launched on Rhodesian security forces by black nationalist guerrillas trained in Zambia. As the guerrillas gradually won the respect and understanding of the rural communities, fighting the guerrillas became more difficult for the government forces.

In 1974, a coup in Portugal, resulting in independence for neighboring Mozambique, helped matters. Rhodesia's eastern neighbor now became a valuable ally for the nationalists, and pressure mounted on Smith's government. In 1975, the South Africa government, frightened at the thought of radical nationalists winning an outright victory, put pressure on Smith to meet with nationalist leaders. The negotiations took place on a train on the Victoria Falls bridge—exactly halfway between Zambia and Rhodesia—but the talks broke down when Smith refused to put majority rule on the agenda.

As the war dragged on, it became increasingly clear that the government could not defeat the combined forces of ZAPU and ZANU. White settlers were reduced to traveling in convoys to avoid attacks, and the government was spending $1 million a day trying to defeat the rebels.

Eventually, in 1979, the nationalists and the white government sat down to successful talks in London. Elections were held and all the people were allowed to vote. The result was a landslide victory for ZANU, led by Robert Mugabe. In April 1980, the British flag was hauled down in the capital, and Rhodesia became the independent state of Zimbabwe.

"I don't believe in majority rule ever in Rhodesia, not in a thousand years."
—*Prime Minister Ian Smith, 1976.*

"There is a place for everyone in this country. We want to ensure a sense of security for both the winners and the losers."
—*Robert Mugabe, Prime Minister, in 1980.*

GOVERNMENT

IN THE TWO YEARS after independence, nearly one quarter of the white population fled Zimbabwe, thinking the country was going to be turned into a brutal dictatorship that would persecute them. This has not happened. A democratic system has prevailed, despite internal divisions that once threatened a civil war, and a government that favors a one-party state. In the 1990 elections, ZANU once again won in a landslide victory.

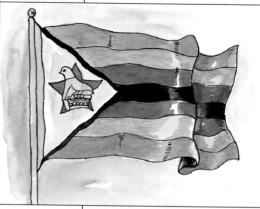

ZANU

The Zimbabwe African National Union (ZANU) has ruled the country since independence in 1980. ZANU began as a breakaway faction of mostly Shona people who were unhappy with the existing nationalist leadership, comprising mainly the Ndebele. Both groups had joined forces in the 1970s to fight the white government, but when independence came, their tribal differences threatened to split the country apart.

Reconciliation and peace came in 1988 when ZANU merged with the rival party, with ZANU remaining the dominant political force. The violent encounters between the ZANU government and Ndebele dissidents are now a thing of the past.

ZANU is committed to socialism, and for many years after independence, Zimbabwe received economic support from Eastern Europe and the former Soviet Union. With the breakup of the Soviet Union in the 1990s, ZANU was forced to re-examine its economic policies. As a result, more private enterprises have been introduced, and ZANU has adopted a more relaxed attitude toward its own ideology. Nevertheless, ZANU is still strongly committed to social justice, and is likely to continue running Zimbabwe for some time to come.

Above: **The present flag of Zimbabwe was introduced after the country's independence in 1980. The black stands for the country's ethnic majority, the red symbolizes the blood shed in the struggle for independence, yellow for the country's wealth, while green represents the land and its resources. The bird emblem is associated with the country's great past.**

Opposite: **Parliament House in Harare, the capital and administrative center of Zimbabwe.**

DEMOCRACY OR DICTATORSHIP

"The government is dedicated to the transformation of the social system, so that the poorest can be included. … There is no inherent contradiction between socialism and market forces."
—Zimbabwe's Minister of Finance.

SIGNS OF DICTATORSHIP ZANU is committed to a one-party socialist state. The reservation of 20 seats in parliament for whites was abolished in 1987. In the period of unrest following independence, there were serious allegations of mistreatment against the Ndebele minority. The Emergency Powers Act gives the government the right to act in a way that would not be considered democratic, and investigations into abuses of human rights by organizations like Amnesty International are not allowed. Television and radio are government-owned and -controlled.

SIGNS OF DEMOCRACY In the light of the former white government's determination to wipe out the black nationalists, ZANU's willingness to accommodate the whites in the process of government is more than democratic. For seven years, they had 20 reserved seats when their minority status would hardly have justified more than one or two. White politicians have actually left their old party to join ZANU.

Opposition parties are allowed, and recently, a new opposition group has contested elections. The Emergency Powers Act was used when there was a danger of civil war. But now that ZANU has merged with the main opposition party, there is a likelihood that such powers will decline in use. Compared to the rest of Africa, Zimbabwe has a good record of constitutional rule. There are healthy signs of an independent press operating in the country. Recent allegations of government corruption were brought to light by a newspaper that was not frightened to speak out. The University of Zimbabwe has also been the source of strident anti-government criticism. Although it has been closed down sometimes because of this, it continues to flourish. Democracy may be stronger in Zimbabwe than anyone believed possible.

Robert Mugabe making a speech to the UN General Assembly on world environment and development.

ROBERT MUGABE

Robert Mugabe was imprisoned for 11 years by the white government of a country he now serves as president. Born in 1924, he received six years' elementary education in a mission school. Later, he studied for two years to become a teacher. During his years in prison, he studied for and obtained six college degrees.

Mugabe became the leader of ZANU because of his radical opposition to the white minority government, and his unwillingness to compromise on the issue of black majority rule. As such, he was portrayed in the white media as a monster and the country's number one public enemy. When ZANU won in the 1980 elections and Mugabe became the leader of the country, there was shock and fear among the white population.

In reality, Mugabe is a mild-mannered and peaceful man who sought reconciliation rather than revenge. In time, he convinced the white settlers that they had nothing to fear, and won their respect. Dealing with the Ndebele minority was another tremendous obstacle for him. Although this took nearly 10 years to achieve, there is now a lasting sense of national conciliation within the country.

Supporters of Robert Mugabe made their presence felt at a ZANU rally held in Harare.

Although Mugabe won a landslide victory in the 1990 elections, his popularity is lower than it has ever been. Economic problems beset his government. And while the liberation of South Africa is welcomed, Mugabe knows it will provide stiff economic competition for his own country.

Mugabe's position as leader of ZANU and Zimbabwe is, nevertheless, assured. He has tried to implement a code of behavior for government officials, to ensure that they do not become rich at the expense of others. History may judge him to be one of Africa's most enlightened rulers. What is not in dispute is that the peaceful development of Zimbabwe, as a stable and relatively prosperous nation, owes a great deal to Mugabe; it is unlikely that it would have happened without him.

THE FUTURE

Zimbabwe is not a one-party state, although ZANU has nearly all the seats in the House of Assembly. Opposition groups do exist, and may fare even

SYSTEM OF GOVERNMENT

Zimbabwe is a constitutional democracy, with a declaration of rights that guarantees the freedom of the individual, regardless of race, religion, or sex. Parliament consists of a House of Assembly with 150 members. Any constitutional changes must have the support of two-thirds of the members of the Assembly. The most powerful political position is that of the president, and Mugabe was re-elected in 1990 to fill it.

better in the future if economic problems continue to hamper progress. Unemployment is growing, and the important land problem has still not been resolved. During the war against the white government in the 1970s, large-scale support for the black nationalists was based on the fact that people were promised a redistribution of land—returning to blacks the large areas of valuable land that are in the hands of a small number of white farmers and businesses. That promise has yet to be delivered.

There was a 10-year agreement made in 1980 that land would not be purchased from white owners unless they offered it for sale. The 10 years have lapsed. During the 1990 election campaign, ZANU announced its intention to speed up the redistribution of land through compulsory purchases. A law to put that into effect was passed in 1992.

ZANU won the 1990 election, taking 116 of the 119 seats contested. However, as is the case with the American democratic system, around half the electorate did not bother to vote.

The government of Mugabe has achieved quite a lot in the face of severe political and social pressure. It has dealt more than fairly with the white minority. In the field of health and education, a great deal has been achieved. Allegations of corruption have been made concerning sections of the government but, on the positive side, such allegations are taken seriously and investigated.

The government's concern for the welfare of its people is reflected in health projects that provide medical advice and assistance to those who need them.

ECONOMY

Opposite: **Zimbabwe has been a constant supplier of gold since colonial times. Here, a gold miner, outfitted in appropriate gear, gets ready to work the mine.**

ZIMBABWE has a wealth of natural resources. Large deposits of valuable minerals exist alongside rich agricultural lands. Agriculturally, the country is able to feed itself. However, there are economic problems.

Land distribution is the most pressing issue, a legacy of the unequal allocation of land that goes back to the arrival of the first white settlers. More recently, the breakup of the former Soviet Union has brought to an end favorable economic relations once enjoyed by Zimbabwe. High unemployment is an example of the country's economic ills.

AGRICULTURE

The land of Zimbabwe, blessed with a suitable climate, is able to support a wide variety of crops. Wheat, barley, oats, millet, soybeans, and groundnuts are all produced on a commercial basis. The most valuable crop is still tobacco, although sugar, tea, and coffee are also important. Other large farms concentrate on livestock, with herds of cattle, pigs, and sheep.

Above: **An aerial view of agricultural lands near Harare. Twenty-five percent of the working population are employed on farms, producing 30% of the country's foreign exchange.**

THE LEGACY OF RACISM

The white settlers came to Zimbabwe looking for gold, but ended up turning to the land as a means of earning a good and reliable income. The fact that the land was already being used by the black population did not stop them. The land was simply taken over, and the people who had farmed the land for generations were sent off to "reserves" —tracts of poor, remote land where earning a living meant hard work under harsh conditions.

There are still over 4,000 of these large white-owned farms, and they play a crucial role in the country's economy. They are all very profitable, mainly because the richest areas of soil were selected when these farms were first created.

Over half of Zimbabwe's population live on land that was set aside for them by the white governments of the past. The land is overpopulated and overused, and there is a pressing need to resettle people on better farms. This has taken place, but to a limited extent, and far less than what was imagined by the bulk of the rural population, who supported the nationalist war against the whites.

The land problem is both an economic and political one. There is an urgent need to find good land for some of the country's 1.5 million unemployed. At the same time, the government does not want to fall out with the white minority by making compulsory purchases of their land.

At times, the problem becomes acute. The land where the blacks were forced to make a living suffers from overpopulation, deforestation, and soil erosion. Irregular rainfall can create serious droughts, as in early 1992, when a drought reached crisis proportions. People's lives were at risk and urgent requests for food supplies had to be made.

In March 1992, a law was passed affecting the redistribution of land. For the first time ever, the government had the power to make compulsory purchases of land belonging to white farmers, and used it to relieve the stress on poorer groups in the community. Although there are grounds for appeal by the white farmers, this law will fulfill many of the hopes and aspirations of those who fought for independence. It should also relieve the economic pressures created by the unequal distribution of the land.

Tobacco is Zimbabwe's most important crop. The seedlings are planted in November to catch the rainfall at that time of the year. Although the seedlings require plenty of water, the soil must be well drained for them to thrive.

TOBACCO FARMING

Over half a million people work on the tobacco farms of Zimbabwe, and the crop is one of the country's most valuable products. Because tobacco is exported, it is a crucial earner of foreign currency.

Zimbabwe's tobacco is of very high quality, but the negative side is that cigarette smoking is a direct cause of lung cancer. Countries like Colombia that farm coca are often criticized for their role in the supply of cocaine, and some say that tobacco farming in countries like Zimbabwe and the United States should also be disapproved. Most of Zimbabwe's tobacco is exported to European countries. However, the European Community is planning a total ban on cigarette advertising, so this may affect Zimbabwe. At the moment, however, the economic benefits of tobacco farming are enormous, and there are no plans to decrease production.

A variety of plants and trees can be found in the Eastern Highlands. This region contains some of Zimbabwe's largest timber plantations and orchards.

RICH DIVERSITY

There is far more to Zimbabwe's agricultural economy than just tobacco farming. When the winter months in the Northern Hemisphere deprive Europeans of fresh flowers, Zimbabwe is happy to meet the demand. During these months, some 300 tons of flowers are packed for export every week.

Softwoods like pine and eucalyptus are grown commercially, especially in the Eastern Highlands. It is said that the tallest eucalyptus trees in the world are found not in Australia, where the tree originally comes from, but in Zimbabwe.

Tea is farmed intensively and the country is now self-sufficient in the crop. Coffee plantations are on the increase. Hops are also grown to produce Zimbabwe's lager beer, now exported even to the United States. When other countries were imposing sanctions against white Rhodesia, the absence of imported wine prompted some farmers to try their hand at grapes. Zimbabwe now produces good quality white wine.

Raising cattle for the export of beef was introduced by the white settlers. It remains an important part of the economy. To black farmers, however, cattle are still seen as emblems of power and prestige, and commercial cattle farming does not have the same attraction as it has for the white farmers.

INDUSTRY

Zimbabwe's mineral wealth and its agricultural products provide the country with the raw materials for its industries. The Great Dyke has reserves of platinum and chromite that will provide a secure future for mining in the country, long after the reserves of copper and nickel have been depleted.

One of the largest employers of industrial workers is Zimbabwe's Iron and Steel Corporation. It employs 6,000 people. The company produces a variety of metal products for use in manufacturing concerns, everything from plowshares to components for locomotive engines.

Zimbabwe shares the huge Kariba Dam on the Zambezi River with Zambia, and the construction of new hydroelectric plants along its rivers will add enormously to Zimbabwe's ability to supply its own electricity.

Most of Zimbabwe's industry is located in the vicinity of the two main centers of population, Harare and Bulawayo, where both have vital rail-road connections. In the east of the country, where important timber plantations are located, the town of Mutare is a hub of commercial activity. Here, a big part of the activity is due to the strategic road link with the busy Mozambique port of Beira on the east coast of Africa.

The mighty Kariba Dam was built to provide hydroelectric power for Zimbabwe's growing industries and expanding towns and cities.

Miners taking a break. Zimbabwe is rich in minerals. Besides gold, some 50 minerals, including copper, chromium, cobalt, silver, iron, and tin, are mined.

MINING

Mining is the oldest industry in Zimbabwe, dating back thousands of years to the Iron Age. Burial sites of Iron Age nobility have been excavated to reveal a sophisticated use of gold. Some of the finds include delicate necklaces of twisted gold and seashells set in gold. Surprisingly, perhaps due to its abundance, gold was not worshiped as the ultimate mineral. Jewelry crafted from iron was just as highly regarded.

It was gold that attracted the attention of Arab traders, Portuguese navigators, and British prospectors and entrepreneurs. The British made the mistake of thinking that an abundance of gold mines promised equally abundant profits. In reality, many of the mines had been worked dry, and the ones that were still mineworthy often did not repay the investment in machinery. One of the early gold prospectors was told of "stones that burn" in the area near Victoria Falls. This was the beginning of a profitable coal industry that remains an important part of the Zimbabwe economy.

Apart from gold and coal, Zimbabwe is also rich in other valuable minerals. In the 1950s, emeralds were discovered and, 10 years later, enormous nickel reserves were found. An even bigger surprise in the 1970s was the discovery of platinum. A modern plant opened in 1992, based on the largest reserve of platinum in the world outside of South Africa.

Other countries in Africa have become dependent on one valuable natural resource (oil in Nigeria, copper in Zambia, for example), but Zimbabwe is fortunate to have more than one. Even when asbestos fell in price, due to concerns in North America and Europe about its effect on health and the environment, the consequences for Zimbabwe's annual production of nearly 200,000 tons of that product were not catastrophic.

A pottery workshop at the Mzilikazi Craft Center produces beautiful figures of animals, bowls, and plates to cater to a growing tourist industry.

ECONOMIC PROSPECTS

Zimbabwe's natural resources and political stability are a secure foundation for future economic growth, but a number of problems beset the country.

Vital supplies of petroleum enter landlocked Zimbabwe through a pipeline running between Harare and Beira. However, attacks by guerrilla forces within Mozambique threaten to disrupt the supply. Zimbabwe is forced to deploy thousands of soldiers in an attempt to safeguard the pipeline.

Reconciliation between Zimbabwe and South Africa is now close at

hand. It is likely that the disruptive forces in Mozambique, heavily financed and armed by South Africa, will dwindle away without the latter's support. This will bring immediate benefits to Zimbabwe's economy. However, with a new rule in South Africa and the end of international sanctions against that country, it will offer stiff competition to Zimbabwe.

Opposite and below: **Whether it is weaving or crocheting, the women of Zimbabwe are very adept at their craft. Their skills enable them to earn a livelihood.**

Unemployment is a major economic problem facing Zimbabwe. One and a half million people out of a total population of 10 million are looking for work.

The urban areas are becoming more and more overcrowded as people drift there from the countryside. The failure to redistribute land on a scale that would satisfy the large number of poor people in rural areas is compounding the problem of unemployment.

Evidence of the problem can be seen alongside the roadways in Zimbabwe. It is common to see workers at the side of the road engaged in small-scale work like panel-beating and working with tin, or knitting and basket-weaving. Most of these people would welcome a job in a factory or office, but for the present, they cannot be accommodated.

47

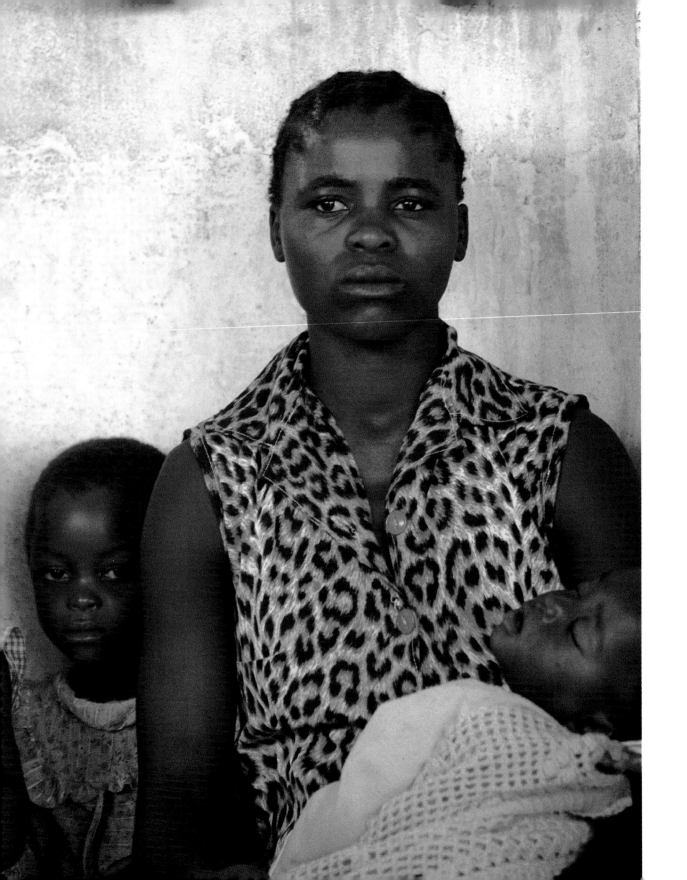

ZIMBABWEANS

THE MAJORITY OF ZIMBABWEANS belong to the Shona tribe. About 20% of the population are from the Ndebele tribe, and they are quite a distinct group. Warriors in the Zulu tradition, the Ndebele originated from outside modern Zimbabwe. The ethnic difference has created difficulties for a nation state trying to forge a common identity. During the first few years after independence in 1980, these differences erupted into violent conflict.

The Batonga are an interesting minority group with a tragic story to tell. The other minority group in the country is the 250,000 people of European descent.

Opposite: **A mother waits patiently with her children outside a clinic in rural Zimbabwe.**

Below: **A group of women and children congregate in a village square for an announcement. About 75% of black Zimbabweans live in rural areas.**

Many of the traditional villages in Zimbabwe are distinguished by clusters of huts made of mud and roofed with grass.

THE SHONA

The Shona people crossed the Zambezi River into what is now Zimbabwe about 1,000 years ago. Forming around 80% of the population, they can also be found in neighboring parts of Botswana, South Africa, Zambia, and Mozambique.

Traditionally, the Shona are farmers who occasionally hunt and keep cattle, not for commercial gain but for reasons of prestige, especially when it comes to marriage arrangements. The majority of Shona people still live in the countryside, but their traditional way of life has been changing ever since the arrival of the white settlers.

There are important subgroups within the Shona. The dominant subgroups are the Korekore in the north of Zimbabwe, and the Manyika and Ndau in the east. Almost half the Shona-speaking people in the south of

Zimbabwe belong to the Kalanga group. The Kalanga are unique: although they are classified as Shona, they are more closely allied to the Ndebele.

The Shona, because of their numerical superiority, are the most important group within Zimbabwean society. It is hardly surprising that Shona-speaking people occupy many of the important political posts in Zimbabwe. The country's president, Robert Mugabe, is a Shona, and members of ZANU are predominantly Shona.

THE NDEBELE

While the Shona came to Zimbabwe looking for land to farm and graze for their cattle, the Ndebele came as warriors. They eventually settled down as farmers, but retained a strong army that was sufficient to deter the first white settlers from an outright attack. The very name of the main Ndebele city, Bulawayo, means "place of slaughter." This is a reference to the violent struggles that took place among the Ndebele for the right to rule.

Today, the Ndebele are still concentrated in the southwest of the country around Bulawayo, where their ancestors first settled. The warrior ethos is now a thing of the past, and young boys and girls no longer have their earlobes slit as a mark of their initiation into the tribe.

Nevertheless, the Ndebele do have a strong sense of their own separate identity. It is expressed in one of their proverbs: "Imbokodo kazicholelan," or "grindstones don't grind for each other." The idea behind the proverb is that, as grindstones consist of two stones carefully tailored to fit each other, it is no easy matter to just put any two stones together and expect them to work smoothly. The implication is that a tribe or culture has its own unique identity that cannot easily be integrated with another way of life.

Although they form only 20% of the population, the Ndebele people have always played a part in all the liberation struggles against foreign domination.

In the years after independence in 1980, it seemed as if rivalry between the Ndebele and the Shona were going to erupt into civil war. The Shona central government sent troops into Ndebele areas to defeat rebel groups that rejected the peace settlement. Terrible crimes were committed by both sides.

In 1988, peace was established and the Ndebele leader, Joshua Nkomo, who had fled abroad, returned as vice president of the country. Today, the peace seems to be a secure and permanent one, mainly because the source of conflict was not really tribal, but more to do with worries about land resettlement. Plans to open Zimbabwe's second university in Bulawayo are under way, a sign that the country's most important minority have become an integral part of its society.

A Ndebele in his straw dwelling.

THE WHITE MINORITY

Out of Zimbabwe's total population of about 10 million, about 250,000 are white citizens of European descent. Most of the white people, who once ruled the country, trace their origins to Britain. In the years of fighting leading up to independence, and immediately after the advent of black majority rule, a large number of whites fled the country. Many of them went to live in South Africa.

The whites who remained in the new state of Zimbabwe were assured that their farms and possessions would not be confiscated for 10 years, if at all. The promise was kept. The large and prosperous farms covering vast tracts of the country's best land remain under white ownership. Around 80% of the country's agricultural products are produced on these farmlands. Consequently, the white citizens of Zimbabwe have kept their high standard of living.

Relations between blacks and whites are better now than at any other time since the colonists first arrived in 1890. Before 1980, the whites convinced themselves that the vast majority of blacks were actually happy with their inferior situation. The reality was quite different. Blacks were not able to vote, own the good land that belonged to their ancestors, or have equal rights in crucial areas like education and health. Very few white people had any understanding of the aspirations of the black majority. Many of those who did, like writer Doris Lessing, left their country and sought a life elsewhere.

Relations between whites and blacks reached their lowest point in the years between 1965 and 1980. Once the white government had broken off links with Britain, it felt free to pass laws that openly discriminated against blacks. In these years, the country came to resemble South Africa, with segregation being introduced into public areas of life.

A white citizen of Zimbabwe whiles away the time at a railway station by reading a newspaper. The white community in Zimbabwe enjoys one of the highest standards of living in the world.

53

The architecture of the Victoria Falls Hotel is colonial in design. Many of the early buildings in towns and cities, especially government buildings, reflect the country's colonial heritage.

Since 1980, the quarter of a million whites have realized that there is a place for them in the new Zimbabwe. The black rulers realized that their country needed the expertise and experience of the whites, built up through years of privileged access to education and employment. The white people who stayed have committed themselves to a new and more equal kind of society.

Old attitudes die hard. Many of the more stubborn whites, who could not accept the idea of equality, left the country. Those who stayed have either moderated their views or kept them to themselves. White citizens who have hung on to the elitist assumptions of the colonial period are sometimes referred to as "Rhodies."

Legacies of white rule are still seen in Zimbabwe. Driving is still on the left side of the road, old British cars can still be seen, and the design of cities like Bulawayo has nothing African about it. Most important of all, perhaps, is the widespread use of English.

THE BATONGA

The Batonga people are a bit of a mystery. No one knows for sure what their origins are. Unlike most other tribes, they have no migration myth, and anthropologists can only guess that they may have come to this part of Africa from the north. Their language does have a connection with Shona, but there is no conclusive link.

Until the 1950s, the Batonga lived peacefully in the rural north of Zimbabwe, in a section of the Zambezi valley. However, the building of the Kariba Dam meant the flooding of their habitat. The Batonga had no choice but to leave their homelands and resettled farther south in the interior.

A Batonga hut is erected on stilts.

Today, the Batonga are among the most poverty-stricken of all Zimbabweans. They used to make a living out of selling their beadwork, but the high cost of the raw materials has made their trade unprofitable. Efforts to improve their standard of living are being made. Money grants have been used to improve sanitation and water supply. For generations, the Batonga were ignored by the white governments, and education was not made available to them. But this is now changing as schools are built in their communities.

LIFESTYLE

MOST ZIMBABWEANS live in the countryside, but the cities are attracting more and more people in search of a better life. In the past, the more productive land was kept for the whites. The majority of the population had to eke out an existence from their poor and infertile land. Things are now changing for the better as schools and clinics are established throughout the countryside, and credit is made available to farmers. But life is still hard, particularly for the women.

LIFE IN THE COUNTRYSIDE

Seven out of 10 Zimbabweans work in the countryside. Even in the cities and big towns, many of the inhabitants have close ties with their families in the countryside. Every Friday, the bus stations in urban areas are packed with people returning to their villages for the weekend. They return to town laden with fresh fruits and vegetables to help sustain them until the following weekend.

Opposite: **A rural woman takes a well-deserved rest with her child. The many chores of village life occupy most of her waking hours.**

Below: **A boy makes his journey home by bicycle. For most people living in the countryside, walking is the principal mode of travel. Buses are used only when commuting long distances, such as between towns and villages.**

Community living is strong in the village, where much of the traditional culture is preserved. However, this will soon change, as more and more people go into the urban areas to work.

Life in the countryside is a blend of the old and new. Farmers use the latest chemical fertilizers to improve their agricultural productivity, but at the same time many cereal crops are still ground by hand. Traditional dress has practically disappeared, but rainmaking ceremonies are still important.

A characteristic feature of life in the countryside is the reliance on walking as the main means of travel. In everyday life, walking is how most people go about their business. Owning a car would be out of the question for the average farmer, since it would be an unimaginable expense. Bus routes ply the roads and serve as the main means of transportation and communication between towns and villages. In the countryside, there will always be a shop within walking distance. The shop serves as a social center where people can meet and exchange news.

A typical farmer often depends on the sale of cash crops in order to bring money into the family. However, unlike small farmers in the United

THE COMMUNAL LANDS

The Communal Lands, areas reserved for blacks after the best lands were taken by white settlers, continue to be home for large numbers of Zimbabweans. Before independence, life on the Communal Lands was extremely harsh. Since the soil was poor, farmers were unable to improve their productivity without fertilizers and modern equipment. But the farmers were so poor that they could not afford these things.

Since independence, measures have been taken to help those living in the Communal Lands. Water pipes have been laid, and grants have been made available for farmers to buy chemical fertilizers. The increase in the farming and production of corn has been astounding. The Communal Lands now produce 12 times more corn than they did before 1980.

Problems remain, however, and one of the most serious is that of soil erosion. The problem is caused by the constant need to collect firewood and timber for the building of homes. What makes the problem worse is that herds of cattle eat the thin grass cover, subjecting the topsoil to erosion. Matters would improve if the density of the cattle population is reduced, but farmers are often reluctant to cut down on their stock.

Soil erosion and drought have combined to drive out people from the Communal Lands. Sometimes these people occupy underused areas on the larger white-owned farms. This makes them vulnerable to arrest as squatters, and increases their dissatisfaction at the slow rate of land reform. They wonder if some of the land that belonged to their ancestors will ever, once again, be rightfully theirs.

States, a large proportion of the food needed for the family is produced on the farm. Corn grown in the fields is taken on foot to the local mill for grinding, and this provides the staple diet for the household. Fruit trees and vegetables are carefully cultivated. Firewood for cooking is also collected on foot, requiring longer and longer journeys as sources become more distant.

A common feature of life in the countryside is for young men to leave their villages to find work elsewhere. The village, however, remains their home, and most have a wife and children there to return to. Out of economic necessity, the men will work as farmhands on the big white-owned farms, or travel to the towns for work in manufacturing plants. Sometimes they will go farther afield, such as to South Africa, for employment in the gold mines or factories.

Goats are raised for their meat and milk. One or two goats can supply sufficient milk for a family throughout the year.

A typical scene in the countryside is that of a woman carrying a heavy basket on her head, with perhaps a young child strapped to her back. Carrying the weight on the head is not just some quaint habit. It actually enables a heavy load to be more evenly distributed throughout the body, and reduces the strain.

Women are more than the equals of men when it comes to working in the fields and running the home. However, many still think that men are the legal and intellectual superiors. Only men can inherit or achieve positions of authority within a chieftaincy. Such views were challenged during the years between 1972 and 1980, when women fought alongside men in the nationalist struggle.

Since independence, the government has remained committed to a policy of encouraging equality between the sexes. Gradual improvements have been made. Women's cooperatives, unheard of before 1980, are now common, and progress is especially evident in the field of education. The availability of schooling to Zimbabwean females has opened many doors previously closed to them. Employment possibilities, however, are not always available. It is still common to find young women, with a level of education that would gain them a place in an American college, working on farms.

MARRIAGE

In rural communities throughout Zimbabwe, as in neighboring countries, the husband pays a bride price to the family of the woman he marries. He then has rights over the woman. She will live in the village of her husband.

When a woman marries, she adopts the clan name of her husband. Clan members claim a common descent through the male line. Although a married woman will use the clan name of her husband, she can never become part of that clan. If the marriage should prove unsuccessful and a divorce occurs, the woman will return to her father's territory and take up his clan name once more.

PAYING FOR YOUR WIFE

The usual practice is to pay the bride price in the form of cattle. For the Shona and the Ndebele people, cattle are valuable for more than commercial reasons; they represent the status and prestige of a family. The more cattle a family herds, the more prestigious it becomes. The handing over of cattle as a bride price represents the man's commitment to the woman he marries.

In the poorer parts of Zimbabwe, a man may not be able to afford to offer cattle as bride price, or cattle may not be available because of the tsetse fly. Among the Korekore and the Tande, payment for a wife is often made by the husband leaving his village and setting up home in the village of his wife. Here, he will work in the fields of his father-in-law for a set period of years. The length of bride service, or *kugarira* ("kakh-ah-REE-rah"), may be as long as 10 or even 15 years.

When the period is completed, the husband and his family will be able to return to his family village. However, if the bride service lasted a long time, the family is often too well settled to move. The father of the wife will allocate land to them for their own use. If the family decides to settle in the woman's village permanently, the event is marked by various formalities. These include the seeking of permission from the ancestral dead of the village for a "stranger" to join the community.

As they venture into the towns and cities in search of work, women are increasingly finding jobs that were once dominated by men. Here, a police officer and her male colleague prepare to make their rounds.

In the countryside, it is still possible for a man to have more than one wife, although adultery by a woman is grounds enough for a divorce. If a woman is widowed, she may sometimes be "inherited" by a brother of her dead husband. This is, however, not compulsory, and a widow is free to reject the possibility of a second marriage and return to her father's home.

The Ndebele people have initiation ceremonies to mark the passage of an individual from childhood into adulthood. The Shona, however, are different in this respect; they do not have any such initiation ceremonies. Adulthood is marked through marriage and the birth of the first child. In this sense, marriage is seen as natural and inevitable, and an unmarried man or woman can be regarded as an anomaly.

In the towns and cities, traditional attitudes toward women and marriage are slowly changing. Even in the countryside, the growth and development of education is helping to erode the once unquestioned assumptions of male superiority.

THE VILLAGE CHIEF

The chief of any rural community holds important social and political power. This is partly because the chief claims descent from the original "owners" of the land: the first people who ever lived there, or the conquerors of earlier inhabitants. There is a very strong feeling that the past is connected to the present through the chief, a living descendant of ancestors who once lived in the land and are now buried in it. Significant sites in a village territory, pools and hills, for instance, are often named after the ancestors. Stories will often relate how the site has some connection with an event in the life of an ancestor.

The role and importance of the village chief, however, has been changing for some time. The European settlers, wielding the ultimate political power, were able to take from the chief the age-old tradition of distributing land within his territory. More recently, during the 1970s, when the nationalist struggle for independence was under way, many chiefs who were unwilling to cooperate with the white government were removed from their positions of power. They were replaced by new chiefs who were willing to support the government. Even whole villages were resettled in the interests of security.

Contemporary life continues to erode the traditional power of the chief. The drift from the countryside to urban townships is gradually weakening the chief's influence. New developments, such as government business enterprises and women's cooperatives, no longer fall under the traditional authority of the chief.

Traditionally, the village chief is spoken of as the "father" to his people, and his ancestors are their sekuru *or grandfathers.*

URBAN LIFE

About 25% of the country's population live in the towns and cities, but many more make a daily journey from the countryside to the urban centers for employment. In the evening, many rural people head back to their villages. As a result, the towns seem quiet after dark. Harare, the capital city, is busier and livelier than anywhere else in the country. Its nightlife is enhanced by the high quality of the Zimbabwe music scene.

During the day, the busiest part of most towns is the market. People come in droves from the countryside to sell their vegetables and other agricultural products. The day's work will begin well before dawn. As early as four in the morning, stalls are stacked with fresh

MBARE—THE URBAN HEART OF ZIMBABWE

First impressions of Harare can be deceiving. The tall buildings of concrete and glass are typical of any international capital, and the city center has a remarkably sedate feel to it. Modern shopping centers, with names like Milton Park and Belgravia, lack any African identity, and suburban areas are still the preserve of middle-class white families.

But a couple of miles away from the city center lies the densely populated area of Mbare. Here, the urban pace of life in Zimbabwe is most evident. Many of the inhabitants are poor, but there is little of the squalor associated with the poorer quarters of other cities. Mbare is home to the country's biggest market (the *musika)* and the busiest bus station.

The *musika* is frenetically busy throughout the day, for merchants in the stalls do not only sell things to the individual consumer. Wholesale, as well as bulk, buying and selling goes on all the time, and porters with wheelbarrows are always hoping for a good tip after helping to transport a day's shopping.

One section of the *musika* is reserved for second-hand products. Here, one can see enterprising stallholders who have come up with a new way of selling something old, for example, sandals made from old and worn-out car tires.

produce. Apart from food, the markets are centers for the selling of hand-dyed textiles and anything else that can be bought or sold.

The markets that dominate life in all the urban centers in Zimbabwe help to foster ties between the town and the country. However, as modernization gathers pace, there is a very familiar pattern evident in the larger towns—the emergence of an urban population born and brought up there. These people have fewer and fewer ties with the rural past of their parents or grandparents.

This is a trend that will continue, and as it does, the pattern of urban life will come to resemble more and more the features of life in any large city. Nevertheless, the distinctive lifestyle of Zimbabwe is still to be found in the countryside rather than in the cities.

THE FAMILY

A child growing up in Zimbabwe is likely to spend far more time with his or her mother than with the father. This is mainly due to a traditional assumption that the mother is responsible for the welfare and education of the children. The Western notion of a close-knit nuclear family consisting of father, mother, and children does not fit traditional African society.

One difference, more dramatic in the past when it was far more common, is the practice of polygamy. A man might well have more than one wife, and his time would be spent among them. The mother's relationship with her child, on the other hand, remains a constant one. Another factor may be the common phenomenon of men having to leave their families to find employment away from home. Fathers leave their villages to find work in the towns, or on neighboring white farms that are large enough to recruit hired hands on a seasonal basis. A young child might not see its father for months at a time.

A typical North American child would have a clear sense of the difference between the intimate family structure and the extended family relationships that include uncles and aunts, cousins and grandparents. In traditional Shona and Ndebele society, the difference is not so obvious. A Ndebele is often able to relate to two "mothers." The natural mother may be called the "little" mother, as opposed to the "big" mother who is there to care for the child whenever the need arises.

In the past, a man's uncle was his "father," and his aunt was his "mother." Cousins were either "sisters" or "brothers." However, industrialization and education have helped to break down such extended family relationships. The term "cousin" is now used in the Western sense, and the same has happened to "uncle" and "aunt."

Opposite: **Mothers have lunch with their children. Traditionally, children in Zimbabwe spend more time with their mothers than with their fathers. This is particularly so when husbands migrate to the cities to look for work.**

Opposite: **Although free elementary education is provided, not all children are able to go to school. Some, like these children, spend their time at home. The boys are expected to look after the cattle and goats, while the girls help their mothers with household chores or look after their younger siblings.**

Despite the process of modernization, the family structure is still a broader-based one than it is in the West. Illegitimacy and orphanhood are not perceived in the same way. An unwanted child would be more likely to find "parents" within the extended family.

EDUCATION

A young person growing up in Zimbabwe today has a very different educational experience from that of his or her parents. Before independence, schools were subject to racial segregation. It was only white children who were assured of elementary and high school education. Christian missionaries played a vital role in establishing schools for Africans, but they were never able to overcome the institutionalized racism that benefited the white population at the expense of the black. Today, around 40% of the adult population have no formal schooling.

The years since 1980 have seen a tremendous expansion of elementary, intermediate, high school, and college education. Free elementary education is provided for all the country's children, and attendance is obligatory by law. There are, however, reasons why this does not always occur. Child labor is a problem in poorer families, and this prevents some children from ever completing their elementary education. In outlying rural areas, there is still a need for more schools and trained teachers. Large elementary classes of up to 40 students are not uncommon, and the student-teacher ratio in high schools is 28 to 1.

Nevertheless, the literacy rate is higher in Zimbabwe than in many other African countries. More and more students are leaving high school with impressive qualifications, although the University of Zimbabwe is unable to offer places to all who are qualified to enter. A second university is planned for Bulawayo.

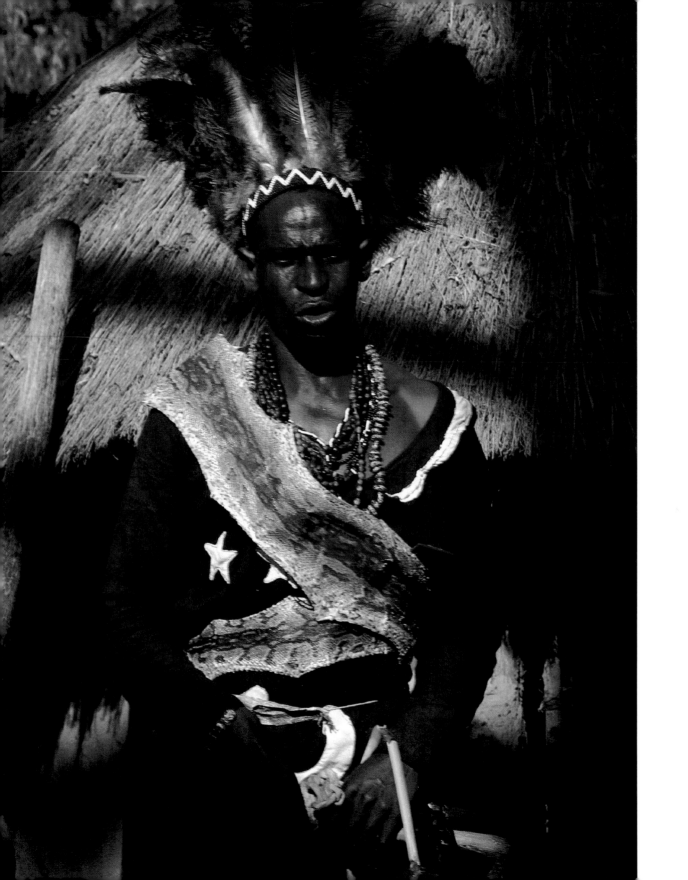

RELIGION

TRADITIONAL AFRICAN religious beliefs are shared by a majority of Zimbabweans. At the heart of such forms of worship is a reverence for ancestral spirits and a recognition of their importance in affecting the present. The opinions of ancestral spirits may be sought in all areas of life. During the war of independence in the 1970s, it was considered very important to have the support of a medium who spoke in favor of the rebellion.

More than 25% of Zimbabweans are members of Christian churches. In the past, missionary churches and schools were enormously important to blacks who were denied a place in the white-dominated society. Many political leaders and prominent citizens of Zimbabwe were brought up as Christians and educated in mission schools. In recent years, though, the spread of orthodox Christianity has declined. What has increased, on the other hand, is the number of independent African churches that combine elements of Christianity with those of local and more traditional rituals.

TRADITIONAL RELIGION

Most world religions share certain characteristics: sacred books, a central store of set beliefs and rituals, a history, and a name—Islam, Christianity, Hinduism, and so on. African religious beliefs and practices tend not to have such characteristics and, in the absence of a name, are referred to as "traditional." The word "traditional" also points to the fact that such local beliefs were in existence long before Christianity and Islam made their impact in Africa.

In Zimbabwe, the creator god is known as Mwari, believed to dwell in the sky above and beyond the human world. Contact with this god is with the spirits manifested by it, and these spirits can take different forms.

Opposite: **A Shona medicine man stands resplendent outside his hut. He may be called upon to cure sickness or exorcise evil spirits by the use of supernatural powers.**

73

On the bad side, a spirit may reveal itself through a drought or some other natural calamity. Generally speaking, the spirits represent powers and influences that humans feel unable to understand or control; hence the need to appease and worship them. Local shrines, such as a cave or a particular tree, are places where it is believed one can contact and communicate with the spirits.

Alongside this belief in Mwari is the belief in the mystical and magical powers of ancestral spirits or ghosts. Ancestral spirits are different in that they were once human. As a result, they are more accessible and understandable. The dead are thought to continue to exist in a land of the dead under the ground, where they are able to keep watch over the lives of the living. If the ancestral spirits are unhappy about something, they are able to send sickness to the living as a sign of their displeasure.

People can communicate with ancestral spirits through various means: prayer, sacrifice, and most dramatic of all, direct contact with the help of a ritual specialist. These include rainmakers and mediums. Spiritual forces can be contacted in order to establish the source of a particular problem. If, for example, someone becomes suddenly ill, then there is a need to find out who in the spirit world is affecting the person's health, and what may be done to overcome the difficulty.

The spirit of a chief is more important. When a chief dies, he becomes a *mbondoro* ("merh-HORHN-dorh-roh"), and is largely responsible for the continued fertility of the land in which he was once the guardian. All being well, the rain will come on time and the crops will grow. If, however, the advice of the *mbondoro* is ignored, or if some terrible crime is committed, then the rain may be withheld. All the men who work on the land of the *mbondoro* make annual offerings of grain at the first harvest.

Shona traditional religion has long been associated with the provision of rain for the crops. A rain-making spirit medium, such as the one above, is a much venerated figure.

ANCESTRAL SPIRITS

When alive, people are expected to care for their families to the best of their abilities. When they die, the responsibility does not come to an end, for they have been turned into *midzimu* or ancestors. As *midzimu*, they have more power than they ever had when alive and continue their roles as protective parents. They can perceive what is happening among their living descendants, and take steps to interfere if they feel this is necessary. They do not act irresponsibly. If they do make someone ill, it would be as a way of signaling their wish to be heard. They might want to warn of some approaching danger, or request that a child be named in their memory.

A spirit medium performs a dance ceremony to establish the spirit's identity.

SPIRIT MEDIUMS

According to traditional African religion, when an ancestor wishes to communicate with its descendants, a woman or man is possessed by the spirit, who speaks through the mouth of the chosen person. The possessed person then becomes a spirit medium.

Mediums are often ordinary people who become ill. Because the illness is not easily cured, it is suspected that a spirit is responsible. In other parts of Africa, the act of possession is spontaneous, but among the Shona, it takes place at organized rituals. The purpose of the ritual is to confirm the act of possession and to establish the spirit's identity.

Such rituals are carefully prepared and often dramatic. Beer will be brewed and a team of drummers booked for the occasion. Relatives and friends will travel from other villages to attend the ceremony, which is usually held over a weekend. Drumming and dancing will call up the spirit, while other established mediums join in the dancing. Dressed in black and white, they carry ritual axes and spears. If the sick person is possessed, he or she will join in the dancing. Later, the one who is possessed will be questioned and, as the spirit speaks, its identity is established. This will lead to the important discovery of the medium's spirit, whether it is an ordinary spirit, the spirit of an ancestor, or a *mhondoro*.

An important medium, one possessed by the spirit of a chief, is expected to look and behave in a way that suggests the chief himself has returned to life. Unlike almost everyone else in Zimbabwe today, the medium does not wear Western-style clothes. The main dress is made up of two pieces of cloth, one wound around the waist and reaching to the ankles, the other slung across the shoulder. Carrying a staff and ritual ax, and wearing sandals, the medium comes to resemble the appearance of a Shona chief. He may also wear a fur hat.

Anyone dealing with the medium is expected to remove shoes and headgear, and is not allowed to carry a rifle. This is a direct throwback to the days when chiefs protected themselves by not allowing people to have weapons in their presence.

Once a medium's reputation is established, he or she is able to practice professionally. Many mediums dedicate their lives to this calling. They will receive payment for curing an illness or bringing rain, but are expected to use most of the money to maintain their shrine. If they became rich as a result, this would lead to accusations of fraud, and their reputation would suffer. In this respect, mediums are quite different from the traditional healers, who are able to become wealthy through their profession. Traditional healers are not in contact with ancestral spirits and are free to conduct their business in their own way. The life of a medium is bound by tradition and convention.

Spirit mediums continue to play an important part in Zimbabwean life. An Act of Parliament governs their behavior, along with that of traditional medicine healers. They are subject to heavy fines if convicted of practicing without being registered. Only authentic spirit mediums are allowed to add the letters SM (Spirit Medium) after their names.

THE SPIRIT OF NEHANDA

Nehanda was a chief, and so his spirit became a *mhondoro*. In the first rebellion of 1896 against the white settlers, a medium of Nehanda played a major part in leading the uprising. She was captured and hanged, but her defiance became legendary. Tales and songs circulated about her refusal to accept conversion to Christianity and the words of prophecy she declared from the scaffold, that her "bones will rise" to defeat the Europeans.

When the second uprising began in 1972, the rebels found that, once again, many spirit mediums were on their side. *Mhondoro* spirits continued the chief's responsibility to protect the land, and the nationalist demands for returning land from the white minority to the black majority seemed the best way to do this.

Later, the spirit of Nehanda resided with another medium, an elderly woman who was weak and frail. Nevertheless, she was keen to help the rebels. However, because of her age and condition, the rebels feared that she could be easily captured and punished. The government forces were well aware of the danger posed by the spirit mediums. They tried to retaliate by distributing tape recordings and posters of mediums who were against the black nationalists.

The black nationalists persuaded the medium of Nehanda to cross the Zambezi River and hide in Mozambique. There, she stayed until her death in 1973. Burial was according to the traditions of a chief's funeral. She was carried to her grave in a white cloth, and buried on a wooden platform that was sunk in the earth and surrounded by a hut built and thatched in a day.

WITCHES

The witch, or *muroyi* ("merh-ROI-ee"), is believed to be responsible for various unpleasant deeds. Witches kill people, turn them into animal forms, rob graves at night, and ride about not on broomsticks but on the back of hyenas. Less dramatically, their presence is felt when a traditional healer or a spirit medium attributes the cause of an illness to a witch.

An unfortunate person may become a witch through possession. If this happens, it is passed down from generation to generation, not only from mother to daughter but also from father to son. It is also believed that a witch may be found within one's own family.

Witches are so feared that death is seen as the only effective way to deal with them. This leads to terrible tragedies, especially as the witch is often identified as residing within a family member. Even today, it is not uncommon to read a newspaper account of such deaths taking place.

The fear of witches is also reflected in the rites that can take place at a funeral. At the bottom of the grave, a shelf is hollowed out. It is on this shelf that the body is placed before being covered with a mat and poles. The grave itself is filled with stones, then with another pile of stones forming a mound on the top. All this is an attempt to make it difficult for a witch to reach the body. The surrounding area is also carefully swept, so that if a witch does approach the grave, footprints will be left.

A Ndebele medicine man's dwelling.

There is even a particular type of song and speech, called *bembera,* that sets out to attack someone suspected by the speaker of bewitching a member of his or her family. Although the person under suspicion is never directly named, the words used always make clear to the local community who is the target of the accusation. The object of the *bembera* is to try and persuade the witch to undo the spell:

"Listen all ye and hear
I am Charungwandicho who cooks even stones
I thought I should let you know that I have discovered the witch
Then don't think I don't know who is killing me
The one who threw sand into my eyes I now know him
Including the reason for my persecution."

An Anglican church in Harare provides a place of worship for the country's many Christians.

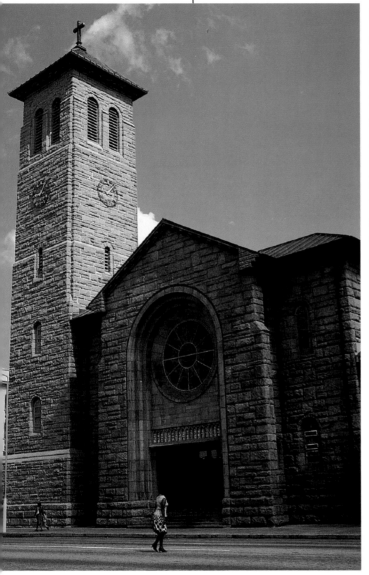

CHRISTIANITY

Christianity came to Zimbabwe through missionaries in the latter half of the 19th century. Today, Christianity has an established role in Zimbabwe. It is the predominant belief system outside of traditional African religion.

About one quarter of Zimbabwe's population are members of Christian churches. Of that number, more than one third are members of independent churches. Of all the Christian denominations, the Roman Catholic and Anglican churches have the largest number of followers. The Methodist and Congregationalist churches are the two most important Protestant groups. Generally, since independence, the growth of Christianity has declined to a considerable extent.

The relationship between the established Christian churches and traditional African religion is an interesting one. Some Christian sects adopt a less hostile attitude toward traditional beliefs and customs than others. It is not uncommon for people to attend a Sunday morning service in a church after having spent the previous night at a possession ceremony. A devotee might have a string of black ancestral beads around his or her neck

alongside the Christian crucifix. In the countryside, especially, a believer would not have a problem attending Catholic services on a regular basis, as well as participating in possession ceremonies and making offerings to the local *mhondoro*.

Evangelicals, on the other hand, are actively opposed to what they see as ungodly practices. The drinking of beer, an established part of possession ceremonies, is banned at church services. Participation in other ancestral rituals is also strictly forbidden.

A pastor celebrates Mass with his congregation in the countryside in Zimbabwe.

A Dominican nun tends to the sick. The first missionaries came to Zimbabwe during the latter half of the 19th century, spreading the faith and setting up mission schools, clinics, and hospitals.

The Apostolic Church is also strongly opposed to traditional beliefs and customs concerning ancestral worship and spirit possession. Founded in the 1930s, it continues to hold the allegiance of many Zimbabweans. In fact, they spend time exorcising the witches that they consider are responsible for all cases of spirit possession. The followers of this faith instead practice what is known as baptism in the Holy Spirit.

Members of the Apostolic Church, known locally as the Vapostori, see prayer as the only remedy for diseases and illnesses, both physical and

MISSIONARIES

Missionaries first came to Zimbabwe with Cecil Rhodes at the end of the 19th century. It was a missionary who obtained for Rhodes a treaty whereby the Ndebele leader Lobengula promised to seek British approval before entering into an agreement with anyone else. The involvement of missionaries in politics helps to explain the hostile treatment they received in the first uprising of 1896. Missionaries were attacked and murdered. The uprising, however, was eventually put down and the missionaries returned. By 1910, there were already more black than white Christians in what was then Rhodesia.

Until independence came, missionaries played a crucial role in providing educational opportunities for the disadvantaged black population. Wherever a mission church was established, a small school would soon follow. Apart from the Anglican Church, others such as the Salvation Army, Catholic, Methodist, and Dutch Reformed churches also set up mission churches and schools.

Many missionaries also established clinics and hospitals. This was often the only way the majority of the population could have access to Western medicine. The missionaries brought many advantages, but they also instilled their own values that were often at odds with traditional beliefs and customs.

Many missionaries came to realize that Christianity was not compatible with the racist society of Rhodesia. This became a dilemma when the black nationalists were fighting the government during the 1970s. Support for the nationalists came from many missionaries. Tragically, many of them became victims of the war. The government claimed the black nationalists were responsible. The nationalists, on the other hand, claimed that government forces committed the atrocities as part of their propaganda war to discredit them.

Today, missions continue to flourish in Zimbabwe. Some of the mission schools are better funded than government schools, and are able to provide a higher level of education. Many of Zimbabwe's leading citizens, including Robert Mugabe, were educated in mission schools.

spiritual. Not only do they reject and oppose traditional medicine, they are also against orthodox Western medical practices. This has resulted in distressing cases where children have died unnecessarily because their parents had refused to consider using available drugs. The Vapostori believe in remaining isolated from society, adhering to their own strict rules. Thus, they avoid the state education system as well as the state legal system. All these have inevitably led to a certain amount of conflict with the government, who wants to see them integrate more with society.

LANGUAGE

THERE ARE three official languages in Zimbabwe: Shona, Ndebele, and English. Shona is the mother tongue of nearly seven out of 10 Zimbabweans, while Ndebele is a minority language spoken by about 15% of the population. While Shona is spoken across the whole country, Ndebele speakers are concentrated around the Bulawayo area and the southwest. The English language is spoken everywhere. Even in remote rural areas, there is usually someone who can communicate in English. In the larger urban areas, English is widely spoken and is the language of road signs and advertisements. Among the middle classes, English is used partly as a status symbol.

Opposite and below: **English is widely used in Zimbabwe, and can be seen in shop signs and buliding names.**

Opposite: **A group of Zimbabweans exchange greetings while waiting for the train.**

BANTU

Both the Shona and Ndebele languages are classified as belonging to the Bantu group. Bantu is the general term for a wide family of languages spoken throughout the southern half of Africa and believed to have a common origin. The origin of the Bantu languages is located in northwest Africa, from where it spread south and east. Gradually, over thousands of years, it evolved into a great number of languages and dialects.

THE SHONA LANGUAGE

Before the missionaries arrived toward the end of the 19th century, the Shona language did not exist as such. Instead, a wide variety of dialects was used that the missionaries found bewildering. It also made their task of teaching the Gospel difficult. The missionaries made a systematic study of the various tribal dialects, and these were later brought together and unified under the common label of Shona.

Today, there are still six main Shona dialects and some 30 minor ones. The dialect spoken in the capital, Harare, and the surrounding district is known as Zezuru. It is the most prestigious one to use. However, Harare is a place where people and dialects mix freely.

In recent years, a novel form of Shona has evolved. It is known as Town Shona or ChiHarare, and is marked by a mixture of English words and Shona phrases. This new urban language also abandons many of the more formal aspects of regular Shona. For example, in Shona, various pronoun forms are used to denote respect when addressing someone who is seen to be superior. But in ChiHarare, dialogue takes place without these pronoun forms.

NDEBELE LANGUAGE

The Ndebele people were Zulus who came during the first half of the 19th century. When they moved north into Zimbabwe, they spoke a Zulu dialect. In the course of time, other tribal groups with their own dialects merged with the Ndebele, and the language evolved its own characteristics. Nevertheless, a Ndebele and a Zulu speaker would have little trouble communicating with each other in either language.

LANGUAGE AND POLITICS

The nearly one hundred years of minority white rule in Zimbabwe has had a permanent effect. English remains firmly established as an official language. In neighboring Mozambique, the language of the Portuguese colonists who once ruled the country still has a presence, but not to the same extent as English in Zimbabwe. The reason for this is not that Zimbabwe has a patriotic attachment to the language of its former rulers; rather, it simply reflects the fact that English is the most important international language. It facilitates international trade and commerce, and serves as a common language for the Shona and Ndebele people.

After independence, however, it was felt that there was a need to register the new freedom in all sorts of ways, and this included language. The very name of the country, Rhodesia, evoked the era of colonial rule. In a way, it even suggested that, somehow, the country had no history before Rhodes and his followers invaded the land. The new name of Zimbabwe, harking back centuries to the time of Great Zimbabwe, confidently asserted the country's new sense of cultural identity.

In the same spirit, the capital of the country was changed from Salisbury to Harare. Some of the important roads and streets in Harare were also

Harare, the capital of Zimbabwe, takes its name from that of a local chief, whose land was seized by the British South Africa Company's Pioneer Column during the 1890 invasion.

renamed, losing their very English character for names of individuals who played significant roles in the black nationalist war of the 1970s.

The names of many towns have also been changed. Fort Victoria is one of the oldest towns in the country, having been a resting post for travelers and explorers throughout the

CHANGING NAMES

Manica Road	— Robert Mugabe Road
North Avenue	— Josiah Tongogara Avenue
Rhodes Avenue	— Herbert Chitepo Avenue
Forbes Avenue	— Robson Manyika Avenue
Beatrice Road	— Simon Mazorodze Way

second half of the 19th century. It was named after the queen of England at that time, as was the nearby Victoria Falls. The town is now officially called Masvingo, although the old name lingers on. Victoria Falls was not renamed.

Another important name change transformed Wankie National Park into Hwange National Park. This is Zimbabwe's biggest and most impressive wildlife park. Other linguistic changes involved correcting colonial mispronunciations. The town of Gwelo, for example, is now Gweru, while Matobo is now Matopos.

CHILAPALAPA

Chilapalapa ("chill-ah-PAHL-ah-pah") is an English-Ndebele pidgin dialect that developed during the colonial era. It allowed communication between whites and their black employees. Most of the communication took the form of orders and instructions. This is reflected in the grammar of the language—the verbs only take the imperative form. There is, for example, no verb that expresses "to leave," only the imperative form "Leave!"

Chilapalapa is still used in some white households employing black workers. It is, however, dying out.

NON-VERBAL COMMUNICATION

Some of the most appealing forms of non-verbal communication in Zimbabwe deal with etiquette—conventional rules of behavior that govern certain areas of social life.

When accepting a gift, both hands may be held out. This is not because more is expected. Rather, it is an expression of gratitude exaggerating its worth. Sometimes the person receiving the gift will clap hands, then hold out both hands, palms up, with fingers slightly crossed to make a kind of shallow spoon. Sometimes only one hand is held out and the other held across its wrist—reflecting an old warrior's show of friendship (not to be seen as taking with one hand and injuring with the other).

Handshakes differ among men and women. Men slap their hands loudly together, with the flat of one hand in line with the palm of the other. Women greet each other by slapping each other's palms gently at right angles. If a very important person is greeted, there is neither hand-slapping nor handshakes. Instead, the men will sit on the ground, clap their hands two or three times, then wait in silence for about 10 seconds before clapping them again for another minute.

Formality governs certain occasions, such as when a stranger visits a village where a meeting (an *indaba*) is taking place. The newcomer approaches the circle of sitting men, squats on its perimeter and claps his hands gently two or three times. At this stage, nothing is spoken. Then the most senior man in the *indaba* stops talking, although allowing the others to continue. The visitor waits for a natural break in the conversation, claps again. If he is welcome, the senior man claps back. This is an invitation to join the group. Generally, a visitor to a village may be greeted by men lining up and clapping gently, while the women express their greetings with loud shrills.

Leaving is also an event. A chicken, a pumpkin, or a handful of eggs may be given as a departing gift. The host and neighbors must escort the visitor out of the village and walk with the person for a mile or so. This is an expression of affection.

Shona children are taught by their mothers how to greet their fathers: by clapping their hands and shouting "Kwaziwai baba" ("Greetings to you, father"). They are also taught a whole series of greetings for grandfather, grandmother, and male and female neighbors. Expressing love through kissing was not common in the past, although the influence of television has made kissing more acceptable.

A chicken is given as a gift. In most situations, when accepting a gift, both hands are held out as a gesture of gratitude.

ARTS

WHATEVER ZIMBABWE LACKS in material wealth, it is amply compensated for by a rich artistic tradition. This covers a wide range of art forms, including music, literature, sculpture, and dance.

Since independence in 1980, a renaissance has taken place as artists working in diverse fields have found the freedom to express themselves. They have made themselves known not only to the rest of the country, but to the world at large. A *manyawi* ("man-YAH-wi"), the spirit of expression and an exciting atmosphere, is in the air.

MUSIC

Music is Zimbabwe's most exciting and accomplished art form. It is not a slave to fashions manufactured in New York or London; it has developed its own identity and style. Some Zimbabwe musicians and bands have become successful enough to tour overseas and impress other cultures with their distinctive sounds.

To describe Zimbabwe music is difficult because it does not fall easily into a category. It is a unique blend of influences from Africa and abroad. Rock, jazz, soul, and reggae are combined with the music of traditional African instruments. The resulting mix has been dubbed "Jit Jive."

What distinguishes Zimbabwe music from other forms is the use of three instruments in particular: the drum, the mbira, and the marimba. Under colonial rule, African music and its traditional instruments were regarded with indifference. Their use was not encouraged. The rules of harmony that characterize Western music are not the ones that underlie the music of Africa. This partly accounts for the neglect of instruments like the mbira and the marimba.

Above: **A masked dance is accompanied by drums.**

Opposite: Sculptures from Zimbabwe are eagerly sought by art collectors all over the world.

The drum is one of the most important musical instruments in Zimbabwe. It provides a dramatic accompaniment to the music.

Also called the "thumb piano," the mbira is held in the hand and plucked with the thumb to produce the melody.

DRUMS

Drums come in all sizes to provide a whole range of tones and pitches. Often carved from a solid block of wood, they are usually decorated with brightly colored designs on their sides. A membrane of skin, made from antelope, goat, or even an elephant's ear, covers the top of the drum. The tightness of the skin affects the musical note, and can be adjusted by heating it over a fire, or by laying wax or heavier pieces of leather over it. There are three types of drum: the high *nhumba,* the middle range *dandi,* and the small *mhito.*

Quite apart from the recreational aspect, drum music figures largely in religious events such as rainmaking ceremonies. Before the adult players begin playing in earnest, the drums are brought out and young learners play with them. It is in such an informal manner that children are introduced to the art.

THE MBIRA

The mbira ("merh-BIRAH") is also known as the "thumb piano." It consists of a small wooden soundboard with tuned metal or wooden strips of varying lengths that are plucked by the hand. In fact, only the thumb is used to pluck the metal. The instrument is positioned between the palms of the hand with the strips pointing toward the player. Mbiras are often used during religious rituals, and the player in a band may be a medium who learned how to play the instrument as a means of communicating with ancestral spirits. In bands, though, the mbira playing is accompanied by participatory voices, drums, and *hosho* (gourds filled with dried seeds). One of the most successful mbira players is Stella Chiweshe. She creates a distinctive style by blending the instrument's music with Western sounds.

THE MARIMBA

The marimba is a xylophone made of strips of wood of varying lengths that are attached to a soundboard. The number of pieces of wood varies from 10 to 20. Being of different lengths, they can produce a range of notes. The wooden strips are tuned by making them thinner in the middle. This has the effect of lowering the pitch. The pitch may be increased by thinning the two ends of the piece of wood. Sometimes, hollow gourds or dried shells are placed under the marimba. These act as resonators to increase the sound level.

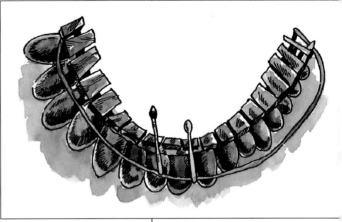

The marimba, belonging to the xylophone family, was introduced into Latin America from Africa.

A marimba may be played solo or in a group. Schools often form marimba bands. They usually perform in community halls and at school events. Traditionally, the drum, the mbira, and the marimba were played only by men. The woman's role was to provide percussion by way of gourd shakers and anklets. Nowadays, this is no longer the case as more women take to playing these instruments.

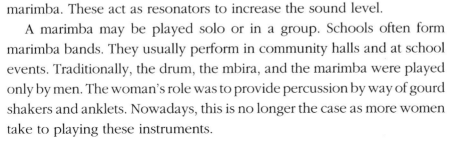

THOMAS MAPFUMO AND THE BLACKS UNLIMITED

Thomas Mapfumo and his band have now achieved international recognition, but for a long time they struggled to be heard. Before independence, Mapfumo made no secret of his opposition to minority white rule. His political songs were not popular with the government. As a result, he suffered arrest and imprisonment. Nowadays, his band produces some of the finest Zimbabwe music. Musical pieces such as *Gwindingwi Rine Shumba* and *Hokoyo* are available in North America and Europe.

DANCE

Dancing in Zimbabwe, as well as the rest of Africa, has similarities with Western dance. In both cultures, dance functions as a form of entertainment and recreation, a display of skill, and as a way of courting and communicating. Both cultures also appreciate dance in aesthetic terms, as an enjoyable art form in its own right.

A significant feature of dance in Zimbabwe is its use as a means of expressing spirituality. The African belief in the spirit of the earth as the provider of fertility is reflected in the nature of its dancing. African dance usually has a downward orientation, with the feet planted on the ground performing firm steps. Often, there is a stamping movement with the knees flexed.

Religious rituals feature singing as an essential part of the ceremonies, and the singing is often accompanied by drum music and a dance. Rainmaking ceremonies also involve dancing. Some of the evangelical churches have incorporated dance into their worship ceremonies.

Dance in Zimbabwe, and Africa as a whole, is often characterized as a group activity. However, in the nightclubs of Harare and other urban centers, dancing can be as frenetic and individualistic as anywhere in the United States. The popularity of live music increases the opportunities for dancing, and the cult of the individual is seen reflected in the act of the single person dancing without any need for a partner.

THE SHONA PROTEST SONG

The modern Shona protest song is part of a traditional genre. Protest songs were once far more common than today. Before the white settlers arrived at the end of the 19th century, these songs were performed before a live, participating audience in the village. As such, they have been called the newspapers of a non-literate society. Protest songs could be used to express a variety of emotions and attitudes. The singer and chorus might express the fear of a parent whose child was suspected of having been bewitched by a neighbor, or joy at victory in a battle, or sorrow at someone's death.

In a novel published in 1979, a woman sings a song directed at her mother-in-law, who has sided with the husband who beat the singer. Part of the song goes:

"I went to fetch water and she said it was unclean
I cooked *sadza* and she said it was underdone
I wanted to be cheerful and she said I was a flirt
I wanted to rest and she said I was lazy."

Dancing permeates all aspects of Zimbabwean life, from religious rituals to political rallies.

In the decades leading up to independence, protest songs were used to reflect the growing political consciousness of Zimbabweans. One song, composed in 1897 in South Africa, became hugely popular in Zimbabwe. It was translated into Shona and Ndebele. *God Bless Africa* became the song of resistance and, on Independence Day in 1980, was sung as a mark of triumph.

Another popular song expressed disdain for blacks who allowed themselves to be used by the white government. Known as *Mr Grandfather-yes-man,* it began with these lines:

"Grandfather 'Yes-please'
You have spoiled the country of Zimbabwe
Everything 'Yes-please'
You are told, live like mice
'Yes master, yes-please'
You are promised more money
'Yes master, yes-please.' "

Sung by a group, the role of the traditional storyteller is taken over by the lead guitarist, with the rest of the group singing the chorus. The participating audience would join in by using the word "dzepfunde" ("zep-FAHNDE"), which means "yes, please" or "go on."

SCULPTURE

Sculptors in Zimbabwe work on wood and stone. The present art form dates back only to the 1950s. Nevertheless, the sculptors have made a worldwide impact. The more successful ones have their work on sale in international art galleries. But for every successful sculptor, there are a

A Shona sculpture, "Baboon," by Joseph Ndandarika, one of Zimbabwe's foremost sculptors.

thousand aspiring artists whose works are found throughout the country in galleries and souvenir shops.

The major sculptors are Joseph Ndandarika, Sylvester Mubayi, Henry Munyaradzi, and Nicholas Mukomberanwa. Also making an impact in Zimbabwe is a school of sculpture known as the Tengenenge. The name comes from a community of sculptors who specialize in carving serpentine, a dull green rock with markings that resemble those of a serpent's skin. The community was founded in the 1960s by Tom Blomefield, a farmer who took up sculpting when his tobacco farm ran into financial difficulties. These artists are open to influences from neighboring states like Mozambique and Zambia. Over 100 artists are associated with this style of sculpture.

Another successful Shona sculptor is John Tarawira, whose works can be found abroad. But not all local sculptors have made it internationally. One major hurdle for many aspiring Zimbabwean sculptors is the high cost of transporting to Europe or North America a piece of work that may weigh a few hundred pounds.

*The first Shona
novel ever to be
written by a
woman was
published in 1974.*

LITERATURE

Long before the printed word reached this part of Africa, Zimbabwe possessed a rich literary tradition of its own. It was an oral tradition expressed in epic poetry that would be memorized and passed down from one generation to another. Legends and ballads were preserved through the centuries in a similar way. The traditional storyteller, the *sarungano,* was either a grandfather or a grandmother.

The first outsiders to take an interest in this literature were Christian missionaries, who were keen to introduce a written language that would facilitate their spreading of the Bible. Today, many Zimbabwean intellectuals and writers resent the way the missionaries rejected many of the traditional religious beliefs that formed a part of this literary tradition, and regarded their actions as another form of colonialism.

Before 1980, a major obstacle for black writers was the Rhodesian Literature Bureau. This was the government's way of making sure that nothing was published that could be seen as criticizing the status quo. Any material proposed for publication had to be approved by the bureau. The effect of this was that very little of any value was published. Writers who wanted to express their opposition were more inclined to use songs and music. During the 1970s, there was a regular output of revolutionary songs that were spread by the black nationalist armies as they moved around the country.

In the years immediately after independence, a number of writers came home from voluntary and involuntary exile abroad. They were joined by writers who came out of the bush, leaving behind them the nationalist camps and taking up the challenge of writing.

Today, writers are seeking a voice of their own. Since independence, there has been a flourishing output of published works in the Shona and

Ndebele languages. There are nearly 200 artists writing in their own languages. Many of them also publish fiction and verse in English.

One of the better known is Charles Mungoshi. He writes his stories in English and explores themes that are common to many developing countries. In one of his stories, a young graduate in the teaching profession fails to see what place traditional religion could possibly have in the modern world. He scorns witchcraft, yet finds himself asking his grandmother for a protective spell. Such a conflict is part of the larger tensions between the old and the new. Education is seen as a blessing, but it also breaks down the traditional way of life and causes stress and strain. The population drift to urban areas is seen as part of this process. A typical character in a Mungoshi story is torn between leaving his family in the village and forging a new identity in the city without the comfort of ancestral spirits.

"Education is a Western thing and we throw away brother and sister for it, but when it fails we are lost."
—*Charles Mungoshi.*

Charles Mungoshi, who writes in English, is one of Zimbabwe's leading writers. In his collection of short stories, *The Setting Sun and the Rolling World*, Mungoshi examines the generation clash, the erosion of traditional values, and the moral corruption of city life.

"The city is like the throat of a crocodile; it swallows both the dirty and the clean."
—Chenjerai Hove.

Above: **A poster of Chenjerai Hove is used to publicize one of his best known works, *Up in Arms.***

POLITICS OR ART

One Zimbabwean writer who is consciously nationalist is Chenjerai Hove. He declares that artists must ensure that "one day we shall dream like Zimbabweans, not like half-baked Europeans." He writes in both Shona and English. His novels that are written in English, such as *Bones*, are still full of Shona sayings and popular myths. Like the works of Charles Mungoshi, his fiction explores the threat posed by urban existence to the traditional way of life.

Other Zimbabwe writers feel that their artistic integrity is best preserved by keeping out of politics. Dambudzo Marechera, who died in 1987, won recognition as a writer while teaching overseas. When he returned to Zimbabwe, he scoffed at the idea of writing to please a political program. In one of his autobiographical works, he wrote about a poet who found himself being rejected by publishers because he was not producing "uplifting" poems that would celebrate the new country. When critics attacked him for not being an African writer, he replied by saying he did not wish to be pigeonholed by way of nationality: "Either you are a writer or you are not."

One of Marechera's poems, *The Trees of the Day*, begins with these lines:

"Trees too tired to carry the burden
Of leaf and bud, of bird and bough
Too harassed by the rigors of
   unemployment
The drought-glare of high rents..."

WHITE WRITERS

When Zimbabwe was known as Rhodesia, a young writer by the name of Doris Lessing decided she could not continue writing in the society she had grown up in. She left her native country and settled in Britain, where she published *The Grass Is Singing*. The novel deals with the experiences of white settlers and their relationships with blacks. Her later novels, some of them science fiction, have not been directly concerned with Zimbabwe.

In more recent years, a new and interesting writer has emerged. Bruce Moore-King was a soldier in one of the country's top regiments, and he had firsthand experience of the horrors of war during the 1970s. Despite the matter-of-fact style with which he describes violence, he is able to reflect on the facts.

In *White Man Black War*, published in 1988, he writes: "I can understand, now, why our countrymen took up arms against us. [And] If these actions and attitudes and forms of selective ignorance displayed by my tribe once caused blood and fire to spread across the land called Rhodesia... Must my tribe reinforce their Creed of racial superiority by denying these, the victors of the war, the basic humaneness of the ability to Anger?"

Raised in Zimbabwe (then Rhodesia) for 25 years, Doris Lessing is an internationally acclaimed novelist. Many of her early works, such as *The Grass Is Singing* and *Winter in July*, deal with the world of the white settlers in South Africa.

LEISURE

IN THE PAST, Rhodesia had a strong interest in sports and invested money in the building of sports facilities across the country. Zimbabwe's governments have continued this tradition. Before 1980, nearly all such facilities were reserved strictly for the white minority, but they are now open to everyone. Sports, for both participants and spectators, provides the major source of leisure activity for a large number of Zimbabweans. Television and beer halls allow for leisure time to be spent in a more sedentary way.

Opposite and below: **Whether it is getting together for a chat and a drink or watching television at home, Zimbabweans like to do things together.**

A premier division soccer match is played at the National Sports Stadium. Dynamos, Zimbabwe Saints, Black Rhinos, and Highlanders are the top soccer clubs in Zimbabwe.

TEAM GAMES

The soccer season runs from February to November. It is undoubtedly the most popular spectator sport in the country. Every urban area has its own team competing in a national league. Rural teams also compete with each other, though not as part of the league structure. A crowd of 40,000 is not unusual, and a really big match in the Super League will attract 60,000.

Another popular team sport is cricket, and the national cricket squad has played well against other international teams. Rugby is another team sport played in schools and at international competitions.

OTHER SPORTS

Horse racing is another popular spectator sport enjoyed by all Zimbabweans. One of the top meetings, Ascot, is named after a famous horse-racing track in England. Golf and lawn bowling are also played across the country.

THE MASS MEDIA

The Zimbabwe Broadcasting Corporation has one national television channel. The resources available, and the common language, have allowed the showing of a large proportion of American and British programs. Although these programs and the ones that are locally produced are broadcast in color, the majority of people still have access only to black and white television sets. Some of the better programs are music videos of African bands.

There are four radio stations that broadcast in English, Shona, Ndebele, and some dialects as well. Radio 1 and 3 are in English, while Radio 2 is dedicated to Shona and Ndebele music. Radio 4 deals mostly with educational programs for schools. Zimbabweans are also able to pick up broadcasts from the British Broadcasting Corporation (the World Service) as well as the Voice of America. Both these foreign stations are only available at certain hours of the day.

Although the government would prefer the newspapers to be more sympathetic to its own policies, Zimbabweans do have access to a large number of mostly independent newspapers and magazines. A popular national daily is *The Chronicle*, based in Bulawayo. This paper achieved fame in 1988 for its valiant reporting of a corruption scandal that implicated a government ministry.

Zimbabwe has a very healthy publishing industry, and the large output of fiction and non-fiction titles continues to grow. A recent phenomenon that has proved successful has been the publishing of works of fiction, including poetry and drama, in the Shona and Ndebele languages.

For the artistically inclined, what better way is there to spend their leisure time than attending an art class?

In Zimbabwe, there is approximately one television set for every 50 people.

GAMES

The array of electronic games that dominate toy shops in North America or Western Europe is not available to young people in Zimbabwe. Nor do the young people here spend a part of their leisure time watching children's programs on television. For the majority of young Zimbabweans who live in the countryside, toys and games are not purchased in shops, and amusement is something that they make for themselves. Children will often be seen improvising

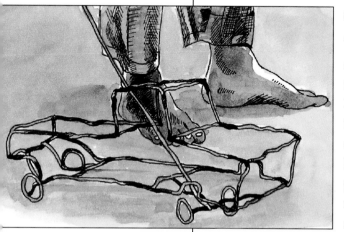

Creativity is the name of the game. Where toys are not available, children improvise their own. Here, a car is fashioned from strands of wire and steered by a long metal handle.

with strands of wire to construct models of cars and airplanes. The finished model, sometimes with movable parts, is steered from above by a long metal handle.

The game of *tsoro* ("terh-SOH-ROH") is played with four rows of 13 shaped holes or more on a wooden board. Each player has two rows plus a set of stones called *matombo,* two for each row except for the second-to-last hole, which has only one stone. The last hole has nothing at all. The stones are moved counterclockwise and, like the game of checkers, the opponent's stones can be taken. Other versions of the game have different numbers of stones and rows. Sometimes, instead of using a wooden board, the holes are simply made in the ground.

The game of *kudoda* (also called *nhodo*) is a children's game played around a scooped-out hollow in the ground about 4 inches in diameter. The players throw a large stone in the air and try to pick up the small stones in the hole, then catch the big stone before it falls into the hole. In other parts of the world, a very similar game, called jumping jacks or five stones, is played.

Mahumbwe ("mah-HOHM-bay") is a housekeeping game played by boys and girls. It is no longer played the way it once was, when makeshift huts were erected and a boy paired off with a girl to take charge of one of the huts. The girl made food while the boy hunted with a spear. The game could go on for as long as a month. The final ceremony included the drinking of beer specially brewed by the girl. It marked the coming of age of both the boy and the girl. Nowadays, *mahumbwe* is more like the "playing house" game, where children take on adult roles.

Ndoma ("nerh-DOH-mah") is a game like hockey, played by both boys and girls with a ball made of wood or root. Two teams compete to try and hit the ball over a boundary line.

A *tsoro* game being played. *Tsoro* is an ancient game, and relics of soapstone boards have been found that date back hundreds of years.

FESTIVALS

IN A COUNTRY where the majority of people still live and work in the countryside, it is not surprising that the most important festival has something to do with the land. The coming of the rainy period is crucial for the growing of crops, and rainmaking ceremonies are the most significant events in the rural calendar. Before the rain comes, the seeds must be prepared, and this can be a ceremony of its own involving the assistance of a medium.

Opposite and below: **Masked dancers at a festival. Dances such as these are staged to ward off evil, pay homage to the spirits, give thanks for a good harvest, or take part in a celebration.**

MAKING THE SEEDS GROW

Before the rain arrives, the village elders and their wives pay a visit to a resident medium for consultation. The ceremony begins with the medium sharing a specially prepared beer with the men, who sit around him in a circle. A small bonfire is lit as the evening meal is consumed. After the meal, blankets are laid out and drum music begins. Women begin singing the words of a traditional song addressed to an ancestral spirit. Others join in by dancing and swaying to the rhythm of the song.

Early the next morning, the crowd of villagers congregates around the entrance of the medium's hut. More singing and clapping takes place before the dramatic appearance of a *mhondoro* dressed in white. After more singing, a meeting takes place where various matters of local importance are discussed. The medium often delivers judgment on these matters, but a more senior *mhondoro* may be called on to lead the rainmaking ceremony that is only a matter of days or weeks ahead. At this stage, money is collected for the senior rainmaking medium.

Agriculture is one of Zimbabwe's main economic activities. A preoccupation with the land and the growing of crops is an important part of a Zimbabwean's life in the countryside. Important events such as the seed planting ceremony will take place prior to the planting.

Once the seeds have been collected from each household, it is the medium's job to distribute the seeds after sprinkling them with various root plants. This will help protect the seeds from pests such as the locust. The seeds are then carried home by the villagers, ready for planting.

RAINMAKING

Rainmaking festivals begin around September when winter is coming to an end and spring is beginning. Without the expected rains, the summer crops will not flourish, and rainmaking ceremonies can continue right through to the beginning of the following year. The year 1992 was an exceptional one, with the drought of the previous year continuing through the first three months of the new year. Rainmaking rituals were extended for a longer period than usual.

A rainmaking festival is usually prompted by the first sign of the approaching spring rains. This is a signal for beer to be brewed. When the drink is ready, everyone gathers at a local spot recognized for its religious significance. The location may be a hilltop, the entrance to some cave, or perhaps a special tree in the vicinity. Rainmaking is a religious event in the sense that ancestral spirits are believed to be responsible for the welfare of their descendants, and this includes bringing the annual rain. If the rain is late in coming, or if it does not fall in sufficient quantity, this is seen as a clear sign that the ancestral spirits are unhappy or anxious about something.

The rainmaking festival is associated with darkness. It usually takes place at night and is characterized by intense singing and dancing. A local medium, dressed in black, will perform the ceremony. Mediums are supposed to be able to make rain appear by hanging out black cloths.

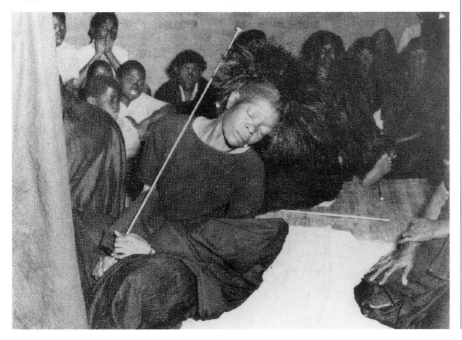

A female medium, possessed with her family spirit, at a ceremony held to ask for rain from Chaminuka, the greatest tribal spirit.

RELIGIOUS FESTIVALS

Due to the influence of Christianity, Easter and Christmas are important religious festivals. Even in remote, rural parts of the country, the existence of a mission will ensure that the birth, death, and resurrection of Jesus Christ are marked by special church services. A dramatic sight in the countryside is the gathering of thousands of members of the Apostolic Church. All dressed in white, they gather in a large open area to pray communally.

PUBLIC HOLIDAYS

January 1	New Year's Day
Easter	Good Friday to Easter Monday
April 18	Independence Day
May 1	Worker's Day
May 25/26	Africa Day
August 11/12	Heroes Day
December 25/26	Christmas and Boxing Day

INDEPENDENCE DAY

April 18 marks Zimbabwe's independence. It is the country's most important civic festival.

The first Independence Day was attended by an array of international figures, including the Jamaican prime minister, who brought with him his country's star musician, Bob Marley. Marley and his band had previously released records with songs that supported the black nationalists fighting the white government.

A statue of David Livingstone stands next to Victoria Falls. A Scottish missionary and explorer, Livingstone spent 30 years of his life traveling and doing missionary work in southern, central, and eastern Africa.

FOOD

IN ZIMBABWE, food has a strictly functional purpose. Unlike, say, French or Chinese cuisine, there is not a deep concern with the aesthetics of presentation. Nor is there the same variety of ingredients or tastes. Nearly one hundred years of colonization have added little to the character of food. The English influence is largely bland and uninteresting. However, like the United States, the quality of meat is very high, and a Zimbabwe steak is one of the country's tastiest dishes. In the capital, modern shopping centers include supermarkets selling the kind of packaged food that is so common across North America. However, for the bulk of the population, the traditional diet is based on corn and meat such as goat, mutton, chicken, and beef.

Opposite: **A vendor sells fruit from the farmlands of Zimbabwe.**

Left: **Salted fish are displayed in rows in a market in Harare. The day starts early here, well before dawn.**

Corn is available in all the markets. It is used in many Zimbabwean dishes.

CORN

Corn is the only cereal of American origin. Over 5,000 years ago, it was grown in Central America. Today, it lies at the heart of traditional Zimbabwean food. Starch is the richest part of the corn and provides a valuable supply of glucose. But corn also contains around 15% protein and 5% oil, and is used as a basic food providing many of the body's essential dietary needs.

Sadza ("sahd-ZAH") is the name of a staple dish that consists of a stiff corn porridge. Every Zimbabwean woman in the countryside learns how to make *sadza,* and knows that cooking it slowly brings out the best taste. In every train or bus station, freshly cooked *sadza* is available.

Corn is also used to make beer. It comes out as a thick white liquid and tastes rather chewy, like runny porridge. Nevertheless, it is a potent drink and retains the protein of the corn.

MEALS AND SNACKS

Apart from *sadza,* a meal usually consists of meat stew with vegetables. The meat itself is often rather plain in taste and appearance, but the range of available vegetables is quite distinctive and adds a lot to a meal. Pumpkin, corn-on-the-cob, and butternut squash are common. The warm climate of Zimbabwe also allows a rich variety of fruits to be readily available. Market stalls are full of guavas, mangoes, ladyfinger bananas, and papayas. Apart from these recognizable fruits that are on sale, there are also various wild fruits that have no English names.

Food stalls and fast-food places serve the usual international dishes, such as burgers, french fries, and fried chicken. Favorite Zimbabwean snacks are often of the deep-fried variety, or the easily made oven-baked sweet potato cookies.

A wide variety of fruits is grown in Zimbabwe's near-perfect climate, such as these papayas on the shore of Lake Kariba.

NDEBELE FOOD

The staple diet of the Ndebele people is based on cereals made into a thick porridge known as *isitshwala.* It is eaten with milk and vegetables. The Ndebele have a long tradition of hunting, going back to the early days before they settled as farmers. They hunt in family groups with dogs, and use special knobkerrie clubs to deliver the killer blow to the quarry. According to tradition, the best meat from a hunting expedition is claimed by the hunter whose knobkerrie or spear killed the animal.

The eating of uncooked meat, although not as common as it once was, has always been a traditional element in Ndebele cuisine. The raw meat is flavored with salt and herbs, and sometimes left to dry in the sun before being consumed. The eggs of birds and hens are also eaten raw.

Hunting wild animals for food was a common practice in the early days. Today, however, many of these wildlife are protected in game reserves and parks. Livestock farming—mainly beef and milk production—on the other hand, has become popular. It accounts for almost 25% to 30% of Zimbabwe's agricultural output.

RECIPE FOR ZIMBABWEAN SWEET POTATO COOKIES

Ingredients

    1 lb grated raw sweet potatoes
    Half a cup each of butter, honey, sugar
    1 egg and 2 cups of flour
    1 tablespoon each of lemon juice and baking powder

Method

The sugar and butter are mixed first before the honey, lemon juice, egg, and sweet potatoes are added. Then the flour and baking powder are added. The mixture is formed into teaspoon sizes and placed on a greased baking tray. After baking at 350°F for about 20 minutes, the cookies are ready.

Whether they are conducted outdoors or in the home, barbecues are popular with Zimbabweans.

BARBECUES AND BREAD

Known as *braaivleis* ("brah-IV-lees"), barbecues are common to Zimbabwe and its neighboring countries. The cooked steak is often accompanied by *boerewors* (an Afrikaans word for a spicy sausage) and a bowl of *sadza. Sosaties* are barbecued or fried pieces of mutton that have been seasoned overnight with curry sauce and tamarind.

In rural areas, where electricity is still not available, barbecuing can take place inside the home. The hut is often a simple structure of upright poles plastered with clay. It is topped with a conical roof of thatched grass. The kitchen area may consist of three stones around a fire to support the cooking pots. With no windows and chimney, smoke is left to find its way out between the walls and the roof.

Bread is baked and eaten everywhere in Zimbabwe. Once, it was made thick and almost black, with all the natural fiber retained. Nowadays, this type of bread is becoming increasingly rare and has been replaced by white sliced bread.

Many people claim that the increase of serious illness such as cancer and heart disease, once quite uncommon in Zimbabwe, has a lot to do with the eating of white bread and other Western food, and eating habits.

The interest in beer goes back a long way. This beer show at an exhibition in Salisbury (now Harare) was held to promote the Castle Brewery brand.

DRINKS

Beer is the most common alcoholic drink found across the country. The canned varieties display many of the brand names that are familiar to people from North America or Europe. Beer is served almost everywhere, including in specialized beer halls and shebeens. A shebeen is an illegal drinking party. In the more densely populated urban centers of Zimbabwe, small shebeens are common.

The brewing and drinking of beer also has an important ceremonial role in all sorts of social situations. In religious rituals involving mediums, the special brewing of beer is often an essential prerequisite. Beer is also brewed and drunk to mark special occasions such as the birth of a child.

Non-alcoholic drinks that are native to Zimbabwe include *mazoe*, lime or orange squashes made from the natural fruit without the addition of sugar or chemicals. There is also the Malawi shandy, a mixture of ginger beer, soda water, and lemon that is always served cold.

BEER HALLS

Beer halls are very much what the name indicates, a large covered area dedicated to the consumption of beer. Unlike the pubs of Great Britain or the beer gardens of Europe, they are not recommended by travel writers as places for women to visit alone. They have a loud and very male atmosphere. Nevertheless, they function as important centers of social life for working-class Zimbabweans. The halls, as well as catering to brand name beers, also specialize in serving *chibuku*. This is the beer that is brewed from corn and served in large containers.

TABOOS ON FOOD

Food taboos are based on the clan system that operates within traditional Shona and Ndebele society. Clans are based on geographical areas. An important feature of clans is that they are exogamic. This means that members of the same clan are not allowed to marry one another. A person becomes a member of his or her father's clan at birth, and there would have to be very exceptional circumstances to ever allow the person to marry someone who is also a member of that clan. It is very possible that this custom evolved as a way of reducing the risk of hereditary diseases resulting from marriages within an extended family grouping.

Clans are named after animals or objects. It is a strict rule that the clan animal must be avoided and never eaten. It is believed that strange punishments will befall the offender who eats the forbidden food. The person's teeth may fall out, or a sudden sickness will afflict him or her.

The taboo on the clan animal is central to the whole notion of clan identity. People, when asked how they know what clan they belong to, may answer by explaining how they once ate some mutton and immediately felt ill. This, they explain, shows that they are a member of the sheep clan.

If a person belongs to the elephant clan, avoiding the animal is more important than the taboo on eating. Another person, however, may be a member of the pig clan. This means a lifelong ban on the eating of pork. Joshua Nkomo, who is the leader of the Ndebele people, does not eat beef.

A possible explanation for the food taboos is that, over the centuries, the custom has developed in order to prevent a shortage occurring in one particular species of animal. If various clans avoid hunting certain animals, then the practice helps to ensure an equal killing rate across a range of different animals.

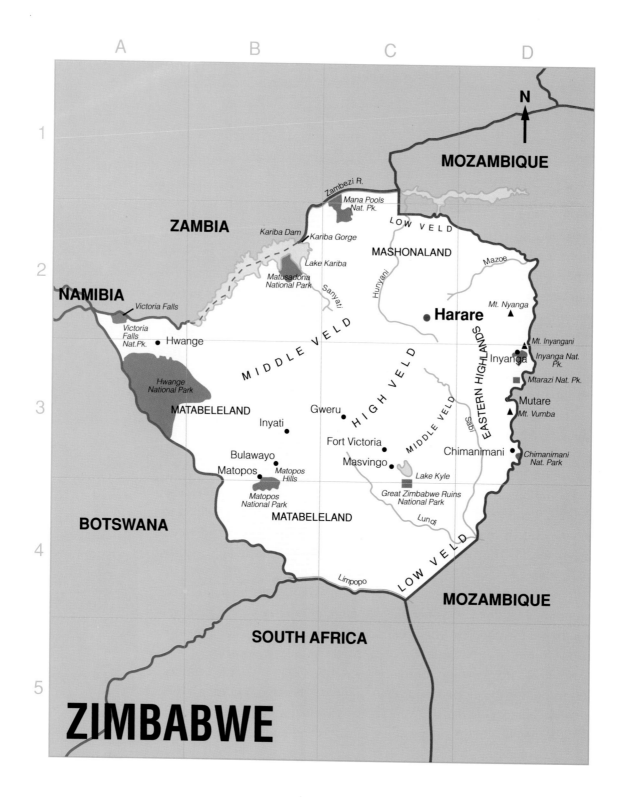

N

MOZAMBIQUE

ZAMBIA

Zambezi R.

Mana Pools
Nat. Pk.

LOW VELD

Kariba Dam   Kariba Gorge

MASHONALAND

Mazoe

Lake Kariba

Matusadona
National Park

Sanyati

Hunyani

NAMIBIA   Victoria Falls

Mt. Nyanga

Harare

MIDDLE VELD

Victoria
Falls
Nat.Pk.   ● Hwange

Mt. Inyangani

Inyanga   Inyanga Nat.
Pk.

EASTERN HIGHLANDS

Hwange
National Park

HIGH VELD

Mtarazi Nat. Pk.

MATABELELAND

Gweru

Mutare

● Inyati

MIDDLE VELD

Mt. Vumba

Sabi

Bulawayo

Fort Victoria

Chimanimani

Chimanimani
Nat. Park

Matopos   Matopos
Hills

Masvingo

Lake Kyle

Matopos
National Park

Great Zimbabwe Ruins
National Park

MATABELELAND

Lundi

BOTSWANA

LOW VELD

MOZAMBIQUE

Limpopo

SOUTH AFRICA

ZIMBABWE

— International Boundary

▲ Mountain

● Capital

● City

~ River

Lake

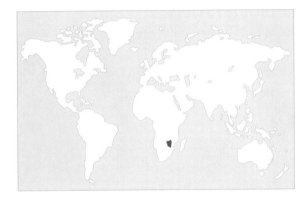

QUICK NOTES

LAND AREA
156,304 square miles

POPULATION
10 million

CAPITAL
Harare

MAJOR RIVERS
Limpopo and Zambezi

MAJOR LAKE
Kariba

PROVINCES
Manicaland, Mashonaland
(Central, East, West), Masvingo,
Matabeleland (North and South),
Midlands

HIGHEST POINT
Mount Inyangani (8,560 feet)

NATIONAL LANGUAGES
Shona, Ndebele, and English

MAJOR RELIGIONS
Traditional African religion, Christianity

CURRENCY
Zimbabwe dollar
(US$1=Z$2.2)

IMPORTANT ANNIVERSARIES
Independence Day (April 18)
Africa Day (May25/26)
Heroes Day (August 11/12)

LEADERS IN POLITICS
Robert Mugabe—Prime Minister of
    Zimbabwe (1980–1987), President of
    Zimbabwe (1987–today)
Joshua Nkomo—Nationalist leader of
    ZAPU (Zimbabwe African People's
    Union) and Mugabe's foremost
    opponent

LEADERS IN LITERATURE
Charles Mungoshi
Chenjerai Hove
Dambudzo Marechera

GLOSSARY

Chimurenga Liberation war. The First Chimurenga was the risings of 1896-97 against the British South Africa Company. The Second Chimurenga was the black nationalist war of the 1970s against white racist rule.

mbondoro ("merh-HORHN-dorh-roh") The spirit of a chief, who may be contacted through a spirit medium.

sadza ("sahd-ZAH") The traditional corn porridge that forms the staple diet of most Zimbabweans.

zimbabwe A Shona word meaning "royal court."

ZANU Zimbabwe African National Union, the present ruling party of the country.

ZAPU Zimbabwe African People's Union, a rival organization to ZANU. Both groups, ZANU and ZAPU, later merged to form a one-party state.

BIBLIOGRAPHY

Mohamed Amin: *The Spectrum Guide to Zimbabwe,* Moorland Publishing Company, United Kingdom, 1991.

O'Toole, Thomas: *Zimbabwe in Pictures,* Lerner Publications Company, Minneapolis, 1988.

Ryan, B.: *Zimbabwe: The Beautiful Land,* New Holland Publications, London, 1991.

Zimbabwe, Botswana and Namibia, A Travel Survival Kit, Lonely Planet Publications, Melbourne, 1982.

Zimbabwe Tourist Office: Rockefeller Center, Suite 1905, 1270 Avenue of the Americas, New York, NY 10020.

INDEX